Conscious Business Ethics

Conscious Business Ethics

The Practical Guide to Wisdom

Wade M. Chumney, JD, MSc

BEP

BUSINESS EXPERT PRESS

Leader in applied, concise business books

Conscious Business Ethics: The Practical Guide to Wisdom

First published in 2022 by
Business Expert Press, LLC
222 East 46th Street, New York, NY 10017
www.businessexpertpress.com

ISBN-13: 978-1-94784-337-0 (paperback)
ISBN-13: 978-1-94781-438-7 (e-book)

Business Expert Press Business Ethics and Corporate
Citizenship Collection

First edition: 2022

10 9 8 7 6 5 4 3 2 1

To my wonderful family that makes my life meaningful:
Tammi—you light up my life;
Morgan—your equanimity astounds me;
Mary—your creativity inspires me;
Gray—your wit enlivens me;
London—you are my sunshine.

And to my mother, Linda, and my father,
Jack, your constant love and support has meant so much.

Description

The case for business ethics is both settled and urgent; we are within an era of human history in which the most influential entities on the planet, businesses, must align their goals with principles of human flourishing, ethics, if humanity is going to experience a more ideal future than what we now know. To accomplish this attainable goal, we must realize that business is composed of human beings, and it is individuals who must make the conscious choice to pursue a more ideal future.

In this revolutionary approach to business ethics, Wade Chumney utilizes his 20 years of experience in the field to synthesize the ancient wisdom found in Plato's philosophy, the modern findings of positive psychology, and the powerful insights of systems thinking to create a new paradigm for the field. Centered around the consciousness found within each of us, *Conscious Business Ethics* provides a practical approach that anyone can apply in order to develop the one quality most desired by humanity in any historical era—wisdom.

This book has the potential to transform your life for the better. The common threads found within all wisdom traditions are distilled into simple, understandable concepts and diagrams that make practical application accessible to anyone who engages the material. As Sandra Waddock, the Gilligan Chair of Strategy, Carroll School Scholar of Corporate Responsibility, and Professor of Management in the Carroll School of Management at Boston College attests: *Conscious Business Ethics* takes thinking about business ethics a huge step forward by integrating ethics with systems thinking, adult developmental theory, positive psychology, and wisdom traditions. Wade Chumney provides an innovative integrated framework for thinking about links between consciousness and life as experienced, outlining how lives—in business and elsewhere—can best be lived and, not incidentally, how businesses can be helped by that integration.

Keywords

business ethics; consciousness; philosophy; Plato; positive psychology; positive organizational studies; systems theory; systems thinking; systemic thinking; virtue ethics; moral development; conscious capitalism; Kohlberg; Ackoff; stoicism

Contents

Testimonial

"*Conscious Business Ethics* takes thinking about business ethics a huge step forward by integrating ethics with systems thinking, adult developmental theory, positive psychology, and wisdom traditions. Wade Chumney provides an innovative integrated framework for thinking about links between consciousness and life as experienced, outlining how lives in business and elsewhere can best be lived and, not incidentally, how businesses can be helped by that integration."—**Sandra Waddock, Galligan Chair of Strategy, Carroll School Scholar of Corporate Responsibility, Professor of Management at Boston College**

Foreword

As President of California State University, Northridge (CSUN), I have seen firsthand Wade's dedication to student success through the implementation of innovative and highly impactful practices that improve student outcomes.

Upon joining the faculty at CSUN, Wade immediately made his mark as a passionate, student-centered researcher. With the support and encouragement of peers and campus leaders, he pioneered new curriculum with an innovative approach to student learning from his research and new paradigm in ethics, ultimately creating a new minor, Business Ethics. Through the support of his department chair, associate dean, and dean, the ethics minor within the Department of Business Law in the David Nazarian College of Business and Economics takes an interdisciplinary approach and a radical departure from traditional business ethics, empowering students to consciously understand how their own personal ethics can drive business decisions and positively impact society.

Most critically, a fundamental aspect of Wade's courses is a service-learning component. This high-impact practice, as Wade has designed it, not only supports students' learning in the classroom but also throughout their undergraduate experience. The service component allows students to leverage their current employment to practically experience what it feels like to engage in ethical action personally and professionally. After receiving feedback from CSUN students, many of whom work as well as attend school full-time, he shaped the service-learning requirement around each student's work experience, requiring them to write a research paper implementing ethical practices within a current or former employer with whom they were quite familiar. This not only retained service learning as a key aspect of the business ethics classes, but it also demonstrated Wade's focus on the student and his interest in refining his pedagogy for the maximum impact on CSUN's diverse, urban population.

Wade's creative approach to ethics is based on the ancient philosophical teachings of virtue ethics, validated through data gathered by modern science. It centers on the self-examination of the individual, encouraging an intention to be the best human being you can be, and thereby able to make decisions that make the world a better place. He teaches students to practically make changes in their lives in order to be successful. This is a skill for life, as well as for business, and it is contained in this book, *Conscious Business Ethics: The Practical Guide to Wisdom.*

Wade created three new courses within the Business Ethics Minor, open to all CSUN students: Corporate Social Responsibility; Ethical and Legal Aspects of Managing Technology; and Business Ethics: Personal Decision-Making for Success. Because one's life and work touches on different arenas, all of Wade's courses take an interdisciplinary approach, including concepts from history, philosophy, psychology, management, and even information systems. Additionally, Wade has also incorporated a component of advising and mentoring to produce undergraduate research in BLAW 374: Personal Decision-Making for Success in Business, yet another high-impact practice in the Minor and another element to enhance each student's academic success.

Wade furthers students' personal and professional success by helping them develop an ethical framework through which they can view their real-world work experience. He provides an exceptional opportunity for students to focus their beliefs, actions, and goals as they seek to accomplish educational success and develop professionally as civic-engaged business leaders. Students of Wade's Business Ethics classes learn how to shape their lives for the better and achieve greater personal satisfaction, regardless of their future profession. Moreover, they complete his courses with an understanding that they can also contribute to other people's success. This approach is in complete alignment with the CSU mission to uplift individuals and foster student achievement.

Through his passionate research and teaching, Wade Chumney has earned the respect of his peers, both at CSUN and beyond. He has written two chapters in an impactful open-source business ethics textbook utilized in major business schools across the country. Wade has also clearly had a positive impact on students, fundamentally changing their lives for the better. With a record of outstanding faculty evaluations by students, he has had a major impact on learning at CSUN. As a former student commented, "Through Professor Chumney's work, I learned how I can change my life for the better and be successful internally. Now I see how I can go about being a successful person in any role I may have in the future, and I see how I can also contribute to other people's success."

I have taken great pride in the growth of Business Ethics at CSUN. Our world needs leaders who are capable of self-reflection and who view their actions through an ethical framework to achieve socially beneficial results. Wade Chumney has demonstrated continuing excellence in enhancing student success through an innovative and impactful approach to *Conscious Business Ethics*.

—Dianne F. Harrison, PhD
Former President
California State University, Northridge

Let's begin with a couple of quotes from a founder of transcendentalism, who traced his philosophical foundation directly back to Plato, the founder of virtue ethics:

> *Every nation and every man instantly surround themselves with material apparatus which exactly corresponds to ... their state of thought. Observe how every truth and every error each a thought of some man's mind, clothes itself with society its, houses, cities, language, ceremonies, newspapers. Observe the ideas of the present day... see how timber, brick, lime, and stone have flown into convenient shape, obedient to the master idea reigning in the minds of many persons .... It follows, of course, that the least enlargement of ideas ... would cause the most striking changes of external things.*

and

> *The ossification of the soul is the Fall of Man, the redemption is lodged in the heart of youth.*
>
> —Ralph Waldo Emerson

Introduction

Over two thousand years ago, a strong philosophical approach toward life existed in the Western tradition. Philosophers of that era did not simply teach approaches toward living an ethical life, they actually attempted to live an ethical life via daily practice on the basis of their teachings. The goal of their practice was to lead a flourishing life. This is the target toward which the text is aimed: a practical approach providing both philosophical and scientific evidence to support the teaching and development of an ethical approach toward business (and life) on the basis of reason. This text would emphasize the fact that business is a subset of life and ethics is about how to live your life. Thus, business is a subset of ethics. Finally, what I find most exciting about this philosophical approach is that it is supported by modern scientific developments in the disciplines of psychology and systems theory.

If my industry experience has taught me anything, it is that any course in which business ethics is taught demands that one learn practical tools for engaging the subject matter in a manner befitting its title. Countless texts in this field of business ethics cover a vast number of topics; very few actually engage the student on a personal level in order to effectuate actual ethical behavior, once the student leaves the classroom and enters the business domain. This text is meant for everyone, from the engaged CEO to 18-year-old college freshmen, and everyone in between. CEOs obviously wield a tremendous amount of influence over their employees and the organization they lead. Thus, they have the ability to not only better themselves but also influence all stakeholders, especially employees, with whom their organization interacts. The fact that it is accessible by undergraduates is exciting because these students are able to be reached prior to their primary engagement in the workforce. Thus, the principles taught here can translate into a lifetime of positive impact within both their chosen careers and the greater context of their lives.

I think globally there has been a shift from reliance on the standard capitalist market teachings that embody a traditional business education.

This text has the potential to participate in this perspective shift and provide a more valuable approach toward business ethics. By offering an alternative emerging perspective within the text, the potential exists to influence the understanding and practice of business ethics for anyone who truly engages this text. This potential should not be underestimated.

There is one critical concept to remember as you engage in the journey toward wisdom: you don't know what you don't know. The first time I heard this phrase was from my beautiful wife, Tammi, very early in our relationship. It really hit me when I paused to consider the implications. There are things I know, such as ethical and legal concepts; there are things I know I don't know, such as high-level math; and there are things I don't know that I don't know, and I have no idea what they are at this point in space and time. But I could encounter something tomorrow and this wouldn't be accurate anymore due to my level of personal development. This is the mindset we should bring to bear upon a proper study of business ethics.

My vision of a business ethics textbook would be one that begins with a proper intention, utilizes expertise to develop appropriate scope and coverage, and manifests as a practical guide for demonstrating one's ethics regularly within any context. The result would be a text that possesses the potential to be a change agent for anyone sincerely engaging this text. What follows is my approach to teaching business ethics from a practical perspective: *Conscious Business Ethics*. This book is ostensibly about the rather dry topic of business ethics. In reality, it's about how to live the life that you've been given. This book is intended for anyone who wants to figure out for themselves the best way to live a fulfilling life.

CHAPTER 1

Ethics

Meaning

I cannot teach anybody anything, I can only make them think.
—Socrates

In its broadest conception, ethics can be understood as how you choose to live your life, the interaction between you and your environment, the art of living. Think about that for a moment. Ethics is about the relationship you have with life. What could be more fundamental, more profound, more worthy of your attention than that? Ethics is how you *choose* to live your life. It's the relationship you want to have with life. This is fundamental and you have a choice. When I truly grasped the greater meaning of what ethics was really about, it fundamentally altered the way I approached my job as a professor of business ethics.

Me

The secret to a good life can fit on the fingers of one hand: fun, cool, nice, happy, real.

When I applied to Davidson College, I was required to write a personal statement about myself. At that point in space and time, I described my 18-year-old self as a combination of David Letterman and Carl Sagan (Figure 1.1).

I didn't realize it then, but I was describing two perspectives (out of three) that Plato utilized to describe the transcendent nature of our life experience: the Beautiful via David Letterman (I felt that my interaction with life should be fun and was drawn toward a playful and enjoyable approach) and the True (an accurate perspective of the context within which I found myself—this infinite universe). What I was unable to realize

4. Help us to know you as an individual. We want to know more about what you are thinking and feeling. You may want to share significant experiences, people and places that have influenced you, or some unique aspects of your outlook on the world. Feel free to do this in a way that suits your personality.

I would like to think of myself as being a very unique and diverse person. The best way to describe myself would be to say that I am a dichotomy. On one edge of my personality there is a comedic, fun-loving character who enjoys this thing called life--and on the other edge there lies an extremely pensive and concerned individual who wonders about many aspects of this universe which we inhabit.

David Letterman epitomizes my comedic side. He may not be your average, everyday hero, but I am not your average, everyday man. Dave has taught me many lessons which I see as being important in life. First of all, he has taught me that one need not be the best looking, most intelligent, or best all-around to succeed in life--one simply needs perseverance and the right mind-set. I have also learned the overwhelming value of humor. Laughter is a wondrous thing, and all of its effects are beneficial. So, if one has the ability to make others laugh, he possesses a skill which can certainly aid the rest of mankind. Dave has taught me to be jovial and have fun, otherwise I will simply become another victim of this hectic, fast-paced world. The final thing that I have learned from this man is to be unique. It is not necessary for me to be like everyone else; I should develop my own style and personality. Individuality is something sorely missed in this world, and Dave has taught me to be just that--an individual.

Carl Sagan would be the man who best represents my pensive side. Reading his book, Cosmos, was one of the most important experiences in my life. It showed me that this planet is a living miracle in an otherwise barren universe. Mankind must learn that we only have one planet on which to live; once we destroy it, we have nowhere else to go. Sagan also taught me that it is my duty to help the rest of humanity. I have many resources which can prove beneficial to those around me, and as a member of the human race, I should use my abilities to aid mankind. Another thing he taught me is the seemingly obvious fact that all human beings belong to the same species. The color of a man's skin should not be the basis for discrimination. Every person on this planet has an inborn right to determine his own fate, and no one should be able to take that right from him. The final thing I learned from this man is the preciousness of human life. If human beings are indeed the only life form in this entire universe(other than the creatures with whom we share this planet), then life is certainly a scarce commodity, and we as a species should do everything possible to preserve it.

Both of these sides combine to form the young man whose words you now read. This is not some well-crafted farce, designed to give you a false impression--its the real me. I honestly do seek some way to benefit my fellow man. The first step in accomplishing this goal, atleast in my opinion, is getting a liberal arts education. For, only through a well-rounded education can one truly take advantage of this world's many opportunities. I stand now, ready to learn--all I require is an education.

My signature below indicates that all the information contained in my application is factually correct, honestly presented, and reflects my own work.

Signature _____   Date January 28, 1991

Figure 1.1 Davidson College application essay

at the time was the profound value of Sagan's moral perspective on life and humanity (the Good) that has remained with me to this day. I had dreams of becoming a (funny) astrophysicist and enjoying my work, satiating my curiosity by understanding my context and, consequently, benefiting others. That last part is the Good, the third perspective Plato utilized to describe existence. Unfortunately, it took me a bit longer to fully understand my relationship to that concept. This book is ultimately the result of that journey.

I never did become an astrophysicist, my Freshman year calculus course thankfully averted that path. Instead, I got Juris Doctor from the beautiful University of Virginia, based in part on an essay demonstrating my service toward others and wanting to amplify that post-JD. During my legal career, I recalled with fondness that essay I wrote for college, and wondered why the context I was seeking to understand (the legal system) seemed so much less fun (beautiful) than what I imagined at age 18. So took some time figuring out what I could do, given my skill set. I remembered that the most fun I had enjoying understanding context was when I was a freshman at Davidson making it my top priority to take the well-reviewed course in Astronomy taught in an interdisciplinary manner by Professor Bob Manning. It was a marvelous topic taught in a marvelous manner by a marvelous professor. It was fun, I believed this topic I was interested in was meaningful, and it was an understanding of the ultimate context within which we find ourselves. I also pursued philosophy courses with vigor and created an independent study titled: Consciousness and Artificial Intelligence. Remarkably, both these topics are of critical import in the world today.

After practicing law for a number of years, I felt the desire for a career better suited to my interests. Given the skillset I possessed, based on the decisions I made that resulted in my past experiences, I sought to reconnect with that memory that resided within my beliefs. After much research, I found a job on which to aim my intention: a college professor. I could envision myself enjoying my work and helping others by sharing my perspective on a particular context; that's significant because it is a place I would consciously choose to spend a significant amount of my time. Fortunately, I became a professor and loved my job, though I was constrained by the context of my expertise (law), and sought to expand that to an area I enjoyed more, technology, by obtaining a Masters in Information Systems. This expanded the context of my teaching and research by forcing me to focus my attention on the interaction between two different perspectives, to look at how they informed each other and, more importantly (and subtly), to look at a larger context within which both were contained.

As fortune would have it, I was compelled early on to teach Business Ethics and as I began to realize the larger context that I was able to teach outside of either law or technology, I was drawn to it. Slowly but surely, I came to realize that this was the ultimate context within which law and technology were both subsumed. This understanding isn't initially obvious, of course, but with focused attention, a powerful intention, and practice, this understanding emerged over time. In what I've come to understand as a very intriguing occurrence, whereas as a college freshman I thought the greatest context was our external universe, I now know it is our inner consciousness that is the greatest context one could hope to envision. It informs both ourselves and our context via where we choose to focus our intention, which will bring our attention and resulting actions along with it.

How does that understanding emerge from a study of business ethics? As simply and directly as I can state it: ethics strives toward an ideal inter-action with whatever context you find yourself. The intent of ethics is to answer the question: how should one live their life? Business ethics is the subsidiary question of how should one live their life within the smaller context of business (which is subsumed within the larger context of one's life). What I find intriguing is that this is exactly the opposite direction toward which I pointed my attention as a freshman at Davidson with aspirations of becoming an astrophysicist examining the infinite universal context within which we find ourselves. The orientation of ethics forced me to gradually realize, by degrees, that the proper focus of one's attention should be an internal orientation.

You

Some see, some see when shown, some don't see.
—Leonardo Da Vinci

This book is about you. It's about the choices you make to determine the life you experience. There exists, within the field of business ethics, a well-established path to a joyous, flourishing life experience, and it is the intention of this text to demonstrate to your reasoning mind why this is so and how to effectuate that life.

A primary purpose of this text is to assist the reader in developing the habit of thinking, via the proper application of reason, for themselves. Everything that follows is based on reason. This is a journey aimed toward wisdom, by application of reason from selfish to selfless, from egoistic to altruistic, from mine to kind. Selfishness is a conditioned aspect of our instinctual selves and through self-development, it can be modified toward better intentions.

An excellent question for you to ask yourself before embarking on any intended course of action is, "Why?" For starters you might want to ask yourself why you are reading this text? You may be a business professional seeking a practical understanding of business ethics, a student reading this text because it is required for a course, a professor considering this for adoption, or a curious person who finds the title interesting. Regardless of which perspective you're coming from, what's fascinating is that the ultimate reason given by each of these various perspectives is ultimately the same!

Take the perspective of a student. You may respond that it is a required text for a course you're enrolled in. But don't stop there. The "why?" behind the "why?" is a critical question to ask until you come to some sort of grounded original cause. You should continue to ask the question until you find the ultimate goal toward which all your actions are aimed. For instance, after noting that the text was required reading for a course, you may then note that you need the course to graduate. When asked why you wish to graduate, you may say to get a good job. When asked why you want a good job, you may reply, "So that I can make good money." Many people stop their inquiry here and assume that money is their ultimate aim. But pressed further, people tend to note that they want to earn good money so they can provide for themselves and their family. When asked why they wish to provide this, the usual response is to enjoy their life.

What should not surprise you is that this is the ultimate answer to "why?" that human beings have given for centuries regarding what ultimately motivates their actions: to have a good life experience. Ethics is the field that provides the answer regarding "how" to make this happen, business is one of its contexts. The key is to: Think for Yourself!

CHAPTER 2

Business Ethics

Meaning

Using the phrase business ethics might imply that the ethical rules and expectations are somehow different in business than in other contexts. There really is no such thing as business ethics. There is just ethics and the challenge for people in business and every other walk in life to acknowledge and live up to basic moral principles like honesty, respect, responsibility, fairness and caring.

—Michael Josephson

Prior to embarking on our exploration of business ethics theories, models, and application in your practice, it is critical to define both terms: "business" and "ethics." Given the power and prevalence of business in modern culture, business ethics is a critically important concept in society today. Business can be understood as the contextual system within which you choose to interact.

The environment of business is an entity we choose to engage with on a regular basis. It is also a component of the larger system of the planet within which it is contained, and the even larger system of the natural universe within which we are all contained. One key of systems thinking is to realize that business is a subtext within the larger context of your life. Another is to realize that your overall intention toward life should remain constant in whatever contextual system you find yourself.

Next, we must define the word ethics. Ethics covers the critical arena of how you choose to live your life; in other words, how you choose to interact with whatever context you find yourself within at any point in space and time. This interaction with your context takes place via your perception. One component of this interaction is the action that you choose to take in the external world. Another component of this interaction is how you interpret the data you perceive. This is a function of your reasoning mind and it ultimately determines both the perspective you have of the world and the unseen intention you bring to bear upon it. Ethics can be understood as how you choose to engage the world around you, your relationship to your context. What intentions and actions do you bring to bear upon your external context? How do you perceive the reactions of the system within which you acted? These are the questions you should engage to truly understand the profound nature of ethics.

Thus, stated most simply, business ethics can thus be understood as how you choose to interact within the contextual business system. Once we realize the fundamental nature of business ethics, how we relate to the business context, we can see the vast number of opportunities to instill the knowledge in both ourselves and others. An obvious application of the conscious business ethics (CBE) approach would be teaching business students at any level, from high school, to college, to graduate programs. This material is ideal for providing the knowledge necessary for individuals at any of these levels to grasp a fundamental understanding of the nature of business ethics and how they can personally apply it to their own lives.

A key target audience for the concepts contained in this text would be CEOs, business managers, and entrepreneurs. The CBE model provides a foundation upon which these individuals can build their organization or their division of the company. Those leaders who, pursuant to the principles of positive organizations, seek human flourishing as an ideal goal would be wise to incorporate the CBE concept into their approach. Further applications of the CBE approach include coaches who wish to instill characters in the individuals under their charge.

Another obvious application of this material is corporate ethics training programs. Ethics personality measures are widely employed in organizational settings in order to gain a better understanding of the human beings companies seek to employ. CBE can be utilized as a tool that allows those who pass through the filter of these personality measures to strive for ideals that can result in human flourishing. Analysis of employee moral development is another measure that is presently utilized in this regard. The foundation laid by Kohlberg in this field (discussed later) can be made more practical with the use of the CBE model. Finally, some organizations attempt to demonstrate to employees what managers' expectations are via a benchmark to an ideal employee. Clearly, the CBE model could provide a foundational framework toward which employees could strive. Additionally, any individual who is motivated and desires to truly engage with the world in a way that leads to a good, flourishing life perspective would be wise to seek out and apply the knowledge contained herein.

Perspective and Context

Values are social norms—they're personal, emotional, subjective, and arguable. All of us have values. Even criminals have values. The question you must ask yourself is: Are your values based upon principles? In the last analysis, principles are natural laws—they're impersonal, factual, objective and self-evident. Consequences are governed by principles and behavior is governed by values; therefore, value principles!

—Stephen Covey

Having now understood the import of the terms "business" and "ethics," let's examine two critical components involved in every business ethics (or any other) decision you will ever make: perspective and context. We will examine each of these concepts in order to provide a greater understanding of business ethics.

Perspective can best be understood as your mindset, the present state of mind that you bring to bear upon any interaction you ever have. It is the internal point of view from which you observe the world. Your perspective can change in a moment based on sudden insight, but it's often set fairly early in life and rarely expand beyond those self-imposed limitations. Consequently, most people's mindsets have become a limited habituated pattern. Significantly impacted by ideas introduced during childhood experience, these become beliefs that inform one's perspective and influences one's interaction with the world for the rest of their lives. The experiences you have inform the perspective that you create, and it is from this position that you observe the world and decide how to interact with it.

Your context can be understood as your setting, the world. Realize that your context changes as you go about your day; you may be at a school one moment, a grocery store the next, and your place of employment after that. All of these settings represent a different context, each of which is a subset of the greater context of your life. When it comes to interaction with these various contexts, many people choose to temporarily alter their perspective by playing a different role in many of the settings they encounter. This causes them to interact differently with their world than they would normally since they are perceiving the world from a different perspective, that being the role they are playing. The roles each of us choose to play not only affect how we perceive the world, they also affect how others interact with the world.

The Business Ethics Triad

The pursuit of beauty is the aesthetic function of societies … most would agree that at least developed societies have made scientific, technological, economic and educational progress. Fewer, but still some would argue that ethical-moral progress has also been made. However, hardly anyone would argue that we have made significant aesthetic progress: that we can either produce better art or appreciate natural or man-made beauty more than our predecessors. The pursuit of beauty is directed at promotion. The formulation of ideals, inspiring their pursuit, and providing rewards for engaging in that pursuit.

—Russell Ackoff

There are two sides to everything: an inside and an outside; there is also the interaction between them. When approaching any business ethics decision, there are three primary components whose interactions you should be aware of. It is the interaction of these that ultimately create your life experience within the business system (Figure 2.1). The first, and most important, component of business ethics is you. You are one reading this book. You are the one making the decisions about which I am writing. You are the essential component of your life and you get to choose how you wish to engage with the world at large and business in particular.

You

Business

Ethics

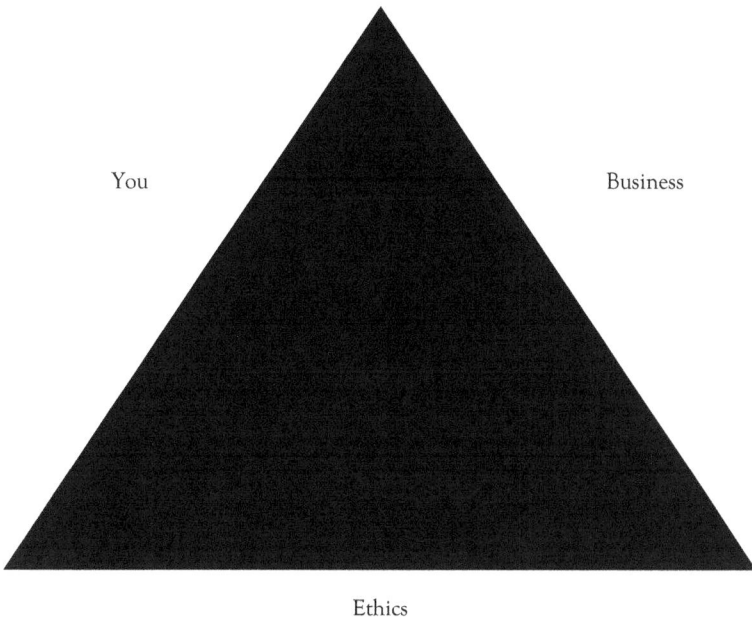

Figure 2.1 The business ethics triad

The second component of import is business. This is the context within which you will be interacting. You will become a component of the business system, which is, of course, a subset of the larger natural system of the Earth and universe at large. The third essential component is ethics, how you choose to interact with the system. The choices you make to decide both your intention and your action are critical for determining how the system will interact with you. It is your interaction with this system that is the subject of the chapters that follow.

CHAPTER 3

Business Ethics

The Normative Perspective

Meaning

The philosopher: he alone knows how to live for himself. He is the one, in fact, who knows the fundamental thing: how to live.

—Seneca

Normative ethical theories were posited to explain how you *ought* to interact with your context, whether that be the smaller subset business or the larger context of your life. They are necessarily philosophical in nature. These approaches, put forth by various philosophers, were describing how you *should* live your life. In modern times, we utilize these theories to explain how we *ought* to interact with the business system if we wish to have a more ideal experience. While other theories exist, the three covered in this section are the primary theories taught in the traditional business ethics curriculum.

As Plato's *Allegory of the Cave* will soon reveal, it always pays to pay attention to the source. So, before we examine the three normative theories most often used to explain how you ought to interact with the business system, we should determine what the source is from which they derive. Tracing humanity's history back, we come to a time period between approximately 800 BC and 200 BC, which the German philosopher Karl Jaspers termed the Axial Age. During this time frame, a shift in consciousness occurred among humanity as transcendent ideas were introduced via various wisdom traditions. These include: Buddhism, Christianity, Confucianism, Hinduism, Islam, Jainism, Taoism, and the Greek philosophical tradition. Note the powerful influence these ideas still hold over humanity to this day. These wisdom traditions express the timeless wisdom of ideal ideas in a form best suited for the context (the point in space and time) in which they were developed. For example, here is a simple easily understood maxim expressed in various wisdom traditions: The Golden Rule.

Universal Golden Rule

Plato

Treat others in the light of the expectation that they will repay good for good and evil for evil.

Buddhism

Putting oneself in the place of another, one should not kill nor cause another to kill.

—Dhammapada 10

Christianity

And as ye would that men should do to you, do ye also to them likewise.

—Luke 6:31

Confucianism

Never impose on others what you would not choose for yourself.
—Confucius, Analects XV.24

Hinduism

One should never do that to another which one regards as injurious to one's own self. This, in brief, is the rule of dharma. Other behavior is due to selfish desires.

—Brihaspati, Mahabharata (Anusasana Parva, Section CXIII, Verse 8)

Islam

Hurt no one so that no one may hurt you.

—Muhammad, The Farewell Sermon

Judaism

That which is hateful to you, do not do to your fellow. That is the whole Torah; the rest is the explanation; go and learn.

—The Sage Hillel

Taoism

Regard your neighbor's gain as your own gain, and your neighbor's loss as your own loss.

—T'ai Shang Kan Ying P'ien

Virtue Ethics

Wealth does not bring about virtue, but virtue makes wealth and everything else good for men, both individually and collectively.

—Socrates

The original ethical theory in the Western tradition is that of virtue ethics, generally credited to Plato and his teacher, Socrates, who left no written record by choice. Perhaps the most legendary of Greek philosophers, Plato also created the first academic University in the West. The virtue approach to ethics held sway in the Western world for over two thousand years. It requires that one be willing to self-develop in order to become the more ideal type of person who makes good decision from a good perspective and, consequently, takes good actions.

Plato taught that using solely the power of reason, each of us can come to the understanding that fairness, balance, is what we should each experience. We each have this basic sense of fairness within us, and we use it to engage with others in the world. This feeling of right and wrong is more commonly experienced as one's conscience. It naturally informs us how we should treat others and be treated, acting as a universal human gauge.

As the name implies, this approach to ethics was that of virtue. Plato discerned that there were four fundamental principles that if actually practiced by any human being would result in a flourishing, happy life. In other words, the practice of these virtues results in an ideal interaction within your world system. This approach can best be expressed by understanding that it requires that you put the four virtues—moderation, wisdom, courage, and justice—into practice. These virtues are the ideal interaction of your body, mind, heart, and actions with your external context. Thus, one should practice moderation within their body, wisdom within their mind, courage within their heart, and this will lead to justice in their actions. The consequence of doing so is that you experience a more ideal, good, and flourishing life. The more ideal experience one would have is described by Plato as approaching the three transcendentals: truth, beauty, and goodness. This approach could be expressed as striving to be your ideal idea of a good human being. If this approach were to be simplified into a maxim, it would be: Be Good.

Deontology

Reason, *in philosophy, the faculty or process of drawing logical inferences. The term "reason" is also used in several other,* *narrower senses. Reason is in opposition to sensation, perception, feeling, desire, as the faculty (the existence of which is denied by empiricists) by which fundamental truths are intuitively apprehended. These fundamental truths are the causes or "reasons" of all derivative facts. According to the German philosopher Immanuel Kant, reason is the power of synthesizing into unity, by means of comprehensive principles, the concepts that are provided by the intellect.*

—www.britannica.com/topic/reason

The second normative school of thought on business ethics is deontology. It focuses on the intention and action one chooses and determines whether an act is ethical according to whether it meets certain criteria. One foundational philosopher who espoused this school of thought, Emmanuel Kant, put forth what he termed a categorical imperative. This was a moral duty all human beings should follow in all interactions within all contexts one might encounter throughout all experiences in their life. The simplest way to state this is that you should act in such a way that it would be good for that action to be a universal law for all humanity to act accordingly.

In addition to his universal maxim, Kant proposed another version of his maxim regarding our relationship with our fellow human beings. He noted that we should:

Act in such a way that you treat humanity, whether in your own person or in the person of any other, never merely as a means to an end, but always at the same time as an end.

—Immanuel Kant

One way of reading this is to realize that you are exactly equal to every other human being on this planet. Just as you have your intentions in life, so too, do they. Those intentions of others should be respected, just as yours should, as you work with them toward in achieving your intention. By this approach, you would never treat a fellow human being simply as a means to get what you want, and disregard their intentions.

Kant focused on three primary concepts to explain his ethical approach: reason, intention, and action. Along the lines of Socrates' approach to ethics, Kant believed that using solely the power of reason, each of us can come to the understanding that we should be fair and just in our intentions and our actions. This is the foundational source of his conception of duty. Since we feel this moral sense, certainly all other human beings do as well. This feeling of right and wrong, of fairness, is more commonly known as one's conscience.

On the level of practical application, perhaps the simplest translation of Kant's categorical imperative is the better known "Golden Rule": do unto others as you would have them do unto you. This deontological approach encourages a more ideal interaction with your context by use of a rule to guide both your intention and your action. It insightfully places the reader in another's perspective, in their shoes. As discussed earlier, playing a role shifts one's perspective so that they perceive and interact with the world differently. By altering one's generally selfish perspective to that of another human being, value and meaning are introduced into the decision-making process. The simplest translation of deontology into a maxim would be: Act Good.

Utilitarianism

The internal sanction of duty, whatever our standard of duty may be, is one and the same—a feeling in our own mind; a pain, more or less intense, attendant on violation of duty, which in properly cultivated moral natures rises, in the more serious cases, into shrinking from it as an impossibility. This feeling, when disinterested, and connecting itself with the pure idea of duty, and not with some particular form of it…, is the essence of Conscience… Whatever theory we have of the nature or origin of conscience, this is what essentially constitutes it.

—John Stuart Mill

Utilitarianism is the primary theory representing the consequentialist approach to business ethics. This school of thought focuses on the consequences of your action to determine whether or not an interaction you have with your external context is ethical or not. Utilitarianism can best be understood in practical terms as cost–benefit analysis. The simplest approach of utilitarianism is to make a list of the pros and cons of each potential action you are weighing. The result of such a list would indicate to you what choice you would make in order to generate the greatest amount of good. The simplest way to evaluate whether an action is ethical or not is to determine whether it promotes the greatest amount of good for the greatest number of people. Obviously, it is hard to measure good and all the people impacted by your decision, and this is one of the drawbacks of this approach to ethical decision making within a business context.

The formal decision-making process from a utilitarian perspective contains the following steps. First, all the reasonable potential actions to be taken should be listed. Next, the various individuals and entities affected by each action should be delineated (stakeholders). Third, the costs and benefits of each course of action to each stakeholder should be determined. Finally, the action chosen should produce the greatest amount of good as determined in the prior step.

Utilitarianism focuses on consequences measured in the material world. Consequently, it is the theory most easily embraced by most, due to its more tangible nature. The most foundational maxim of this approach can be understood as this: act in such a way that you create the greatest good for the greatest number of people. This outcome could arguably be equated with the "common good." It should be noted that measuring good is not necessarily an easy thing to do. If you were to simplify this approach even further into maxim, it would be to: Create Good.

The Normative Ethics Triad

The pursuit of the good is the ethical-moral function of societies. It is directed at removing conflict within individuals (peace of mind) and between individuals (peace on Earth), and promoting cooperation between them. Unless conflict within and between individuals is removed, and cooperation among them promoted, progress toward the attainment of some objectives is not possible.

—Russell Ackoff

Interestingly, the three normative theories that seek to explain how we ought to act in a business context comport with three aforementioned components of the business ethics triad (Figure 3.1). "You" can best be understood via the normative theory of deontology, which focuses on your two outputs: your intention and your action. "Business" as an external context can best be understood by reference to utilitarianism and its focus on generating good consequences. Finally, "Ethics" can best be understood by tracing the three normative theories to their root source in the Western tradition, virtue ethics.

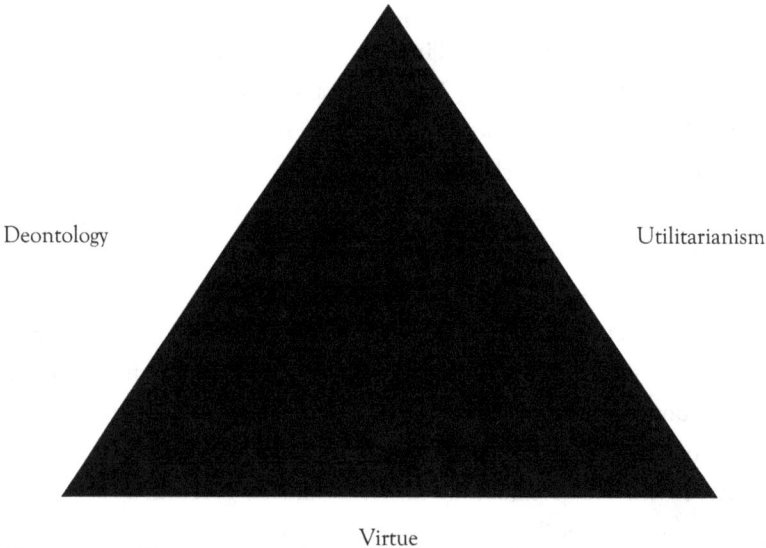

Deontology   Utilitarianism

Virtue
Figure 3.1 The normative business ethics triad

All three normative theories generally covered in the business ethics curriculum converge at an ideal toward which they all intend: Good. This is the coin of the realm. Each of these theories strive toward generating the greatest amount of good. Utilitarianism informs us to create the "greatest good," deontology teaches us to "act good," and virtue ethics inspires us to "be good."

CHAPTER 4

Business Ethics

The Descriptive Perspective

Meaning

The information we allow into consciousness becomes extremely important; it is, in fact, what determines the content and the quality of life.
—Mihaly Csikszentmihalyi

Having examined the principal foundations behind business ethics, and the relationship among the normative theories that inform us how we ought to act, we now turn to science and the descriptive theories that provide data we can use to inform ourselves as to how business ethics actually functions in the real world. Descriptive business ethics utilizes data gathered from the findings of science in order to help us understand how to have an ideal interaction with the business context. Rather than focus on how we *ought* to act, descriptive theories focus on how we *do* act. The actions that we do take are then transformed into data that is analyzed and studied in order to better effectuate business ethics.

Psychology

The chief task in life is simply this: to identify and separate matters so that I can say clearly to myself which are externals not under my control, and which have to do with the choices I actually control.
—Epictetus

Moral Reasoning

> *My own work has focused ... on the deontological approach to moral-*
> *ity ... we have to develop the competence of moral judgment... a stage*
> *increase in judgments of justice. And second, to develop the capacity*
> *and motivation for moral action, which we view primarily as acting*
> *responsibly ... we assume the motivation for the development of mak-*
> *ing judgments themselves is largely based on the internal cognitive*
> *moral conflict, and to adapt to the world by role-taking or taking*
> *into account the moral or social perspective of others ... Reference to*
> *judgments of conscience was one necessary condition .... Another was*
> *a sense of categorical duty in the sense of Kant.*
>
> —Lawrence Kohlberg

Lawrence Kohlberg studied people and the decisions they made in order to determine their level of moral development based on their moral reasoning. His research showed that people begin at the preconventional level of moral development and most develop to the conventional level. But 20 percent of the population makes the choice to develop morally beyond societal norms and reasons at the postconventional stage. Table 4.1 briefly explains Kohlberg's stages of moral development. The key concept that enables one to move up to higher levels of moral reasoning is the aforementioned concepts of role-taking, the ability to reason about the perspective of another human being, and emotionally resonate with them.

Table 4.1 Kohlberg's stages of moral development

Kohlberg's Stages of Moral Development		
Transcendental Morality	7	Actions based on the natural law and agape.
Postconventional Morality	6	Actions based on internal moral law (conscience).
	5	Actions based on principles of human rights.
Conventional Morality	4	Actions based on conformity to systemic social order.
	3	Actions based on social conformity.
Preconventional Morality	2	Actions based on self-interest.
	1	Actions based on avoiding punishment.

It is easiest to understand these stages of moral development by real-izing what provides meaning at each level.

Preconventional

This level of development can be understood as one's reasoning being primarily motivated by selfish instinctual desires. In fact, it is selfishness that provides meaning. Stage 1 is dominated by fear as one seeks to avoid punishment. Greater physical power is indicative of whose view is correct. Reason is hardly engaged at this level and it is expressed as obedience to a greater authority. Stage 2 represents the utilization of reason to fulfill one's selfish desires. There is a greater realization that other perspectives exist and by fulfilling the expectations of others, you can obtain what you desire.

Conventional

At the conventional level, it is conformity to outside standards that pro-vides meaning. In this level of moral development, one focuses their attention outward and utilizes reason to determine a course of conduct that best positions one within the norm of their perceived peer group. Stage 3 encourages one to conform to the group of people with whom they share beliefs and tends to lead to allegiance to either a family or other small group. At Stage 4, a societal perspective is taken. One realizes that legal rules permit society to function. Thus, one expands the scope of their conformity to national laws and customs, as one determines how their role fits into the existing system.

As the name indicates, norms are the typical, normal result. We can relate this concept back to Kohlberg and realize that norms constitute moral development at Levels 3 and 4. Cultures are the embodiment of the norms of a certain society. Culture is designed for the purpose of creating a norm in order to maximize conformity. What is unfortunate about this creation is that while it seeks both to raise the behavior of those who are damaging, it also diminishes the actions of those who are excellent. Those who conform to societal norms view both the lesser and the greater as improper. The problem, of course, is that while society may need to drag the less developed individual along and bring him up to conventional expectations, the greater individual is setting the more ideal future direction toward which social norms should strive.

Postconventional

Natural principles provide meaning at this level. At this level, one turns their attention inward and focuses on the relationship between themselves and their greater, transcendental context. By doing so, one is able to gain a broader perspective that allows them to choose how to interact with their external context on the basis of principles that form the basis of societal formation (think of those principles that undergird the Declaration of Independence). The postconventional level is where one actually practices the process of self-reflection necessary to develop a perspective based on ideals, as opposed to societal norms. Stage 5 can be understood as first time one looks deeply within themselves to determine moral development, and not external social or societal norms. They develop an understanding of those natural principles that inform our development. Stage 6 can be understood as the attainment of Wisdom, alignment with the universal laws of one's conscience. This is when one puts into practice the virtues and experiences a more ideal relationship with their context.

Based on Kohlberg's research, each person perceives the world differently based on their beliefs. This happens automatically because our beliefs inform our perspective. Thus, to change one's belief, the most effective prescription is self-reflection. Stop and think about the internal aspects of your experience and their relationship to all things. Turn your attention inward and focus on your beliefs. Notice the relationship between those and your experiences.

Stage 7

This is the highest level posited by Kohlberg and it is understood as being a transcendent experience. The individuals Kohlberg cites as attaining this level (Socrates, Marcus Aerulius, and Spinoza) are those who were living examples of the ideal idea of a good human being. These exemplars derived meaning by living a good life and sharing that good with others. These individuals have gone beyond the context most of us find ourselves in. They align their perspective with the unifying source from which all life flows. Kohlberg describes this stage as "an ethic of responsible universal love, service, or sacrifice, an ethic of supererogation" (Kohlberg and Power, Moral Development, Religious Thinking, and the Question of a Seventh Stage). Interestingly, this stage can be understood, like Stage 1, as obedience to authority, though at Stage 7 this authority is transcendent and found within one's self.

From an internal perspective, the progression upward on Kohlberg's model can be understood as gaining a greater perspective. Context is the flip side of perspective; it is what you believe your setting to be. So, to simplify Kohlberg's remarkable findings into two core principles, they would be the aforementioned concepts of perspective and context. Furthermore, note that your level of moral development is not an accident, it is a choice. You can choose how to process the data that you perceive. Finally, you should realize the trend of moral development as an intentional movement toward an ideal. Table 4.2 shows the simplified descriptions that correlate with each stage of moral development.

Table 4.2 Stages of moral development and their descriptions

Moral Development	Description
Preconventional 1	Fear
2	Attention
Conventional 3	Belief Conformity
4	Societal Conformity
Postconventional 5	Unifying Principles
6	Conscience
Ideal 7	Transcendence

Positive Psychology

Wisdom largely emerges from reflection on experience. Wisdom involves nuanced thinking, considering many different perspectives .... Wise people are also open to new ways of thinking, challenging the status quo to produce a novel or unexpected outcome .... Balance is a key component of wisdom .... Wise people generally act on behalf of the common good but also ensure that their own needs are met, striving for harmony among competing demands and goals. Wise people may also seek to understand the motives of others .... In addition to fostering understanding and respect of others, wisdom often provides a fulfilling sense of purpose in life.

—www.psychologytoday.com/us/basics/wisdom

In modern times, the science of psychology has taken a primary role in understanding one's inner (mental and emotional) world. Research in this field, specifically with the discipline of positive psychology has led to the distillation of six character traits that are most essential to a flourishing life. Surveying world's wisdom traditions, researchers in the field found six foundational character traits arise: the four virtues discovered by Plato (wisdom, courage, moderation, and justice), along with humanity and transcendence.

As discussed earlier, human beings almost universally intend to experience a good and joyous life. Greek philosophers referred to this as eudemonia, commonly translated into a "flourishing life." Modern science, in the form of positive psychology, has embraced this intention and sought to answer the how by operationalizing the psychological mechanisms involved in accomplishing such a task. Table 4.3 presents a list of these virtues with their character trait subcomponents.

Table 4.3 VIA classification of character strengths and virtues

VIA Classification of Character Strengths and Virtues					
The Character Strengths of a Flourishing Life					
Wisdom	Courage	Humanity	Justice	Temperance	Transcendence
Creativity	Bravery	Love	Teamwork	Forgiveness	Appreciation of Beauty and Excellence
Curiosity	Perseverance	Kindness	Fairness	Humility	Gratitude
Judgment	Honesty	Social Intelligence	Leadership	Prudence	Hope
Love of Learning	Zest			Self-Regulation	Humor
Perspective					Spirituality

A good life experience is created when one chooses to consistently develop and apply the six virtues to their own life. Moderation is the proper use of reason to control the desires and fears that tend to be the guiding force behind the physical actions of one's body. Justice is the proper use of reason to take actions that are fair and balanced within your context. Wisdom is the choice to develop one's reason in order to gain a proper understanding of life, so that you can experience an ideal interaction with your context. Humanity is a deep respect for each and every human being you interact with (and even those you don't), based on an understanding that each of us is the same, a sliver of consciousness having a life experience. Courage is the ability to persevere through the difficulties you experience in life while maintaining your positive intention. Transcendence is the emotional experience engendered from intending toward the Good, often expressed as gratitude.

Systems

Then as to wisdom, do you observe how our law from the very first made a study of the whole order of things ... out of these divine elements deriving what was needful for human life.

—Plato

Systems Theory

Business and other human endeavors are also systems. They, too, are bound by invisible fabrics of interrelated actions, which often take years to fully play out their effects on each other. Since we are part of that lacework ourselves, it's doubly hard to see the whole pattern of change. Instead, we tend to focus on isolated parts of the system, and wonder why our deepest problems never seems to get solved.

—Peter Senge

Just as Lawrence Kohlberg revolutionized our understanding of human beings with the science of psychology and his lifelong study of moral development, Russell Ackoff revolutionized our understanding of business with the science of systems and his lifelong study of idealizing systems. Ackoff noted that our entire culture, including universities and businesses, was built upon the scientific method. This involved a three-step process called analysis: (1) take it apart, (2) try to understand what each part does, and (3) combine an understanding of the parts into an understanding of the whole. The problem, Ackoff noted, was that the product of analysis was how things work, not why they work the way that they do. Analysis focuses your attention inside the system and creates knowledge, but not understanding.

Ackoff put forth another way of thinking about how a system behaves: synthesis. Synthesis consists of three steps, which are the opposite of analysis: (1) identify the larger system of which this is a part, (2) try to understand the behavior of the whole system, and (3) identify the role of the component that I am trying to explain within that whole. Pursuant to Ackoff, a system can be understood as a whole that is defined by its role within the larger system of which it is a part. All systems are contained within larger systems, and its role within that larger system is what defines it. For a system to perform its role, it has essential parts; these are necessary for the system to perform its role but not sufficient. In other words, the essential parts are required for the system to function properly, but more is needed. One property of a system is that it cannot be divided into independent parts. The properties of a system derive from the interaction of its parts, not the actions of its component parts taken separately. Thus, if you apply analytical thinking to a system, you take it apart and the system loses all of its essential properties, as do its parts. Consequently, a system can never be the sum of its parts; it is the product of the interactions of its parts.

Learning

> *Much like the meaning it carries in a mathematical context which is simply a synonym for the number "one," Unity in systems thinking actually just means " Oneness" or " the whole." This meaning of unity in systems thinking is more a matter of fact than a potential state of being. This concept of oneness is a foundational principle of any systems thinking analysis and it frames the systems thinking worldview through which we look at organisations, eco-systems, societies and families.*
> —https://erfandaliri.com/blog/unityandsystemsthinking

In order to explain the learning process of organizations, and individuals, Ackoff posited five types of learning: data, information, knowledge, understanding, and wisdom (Figure 4.1). He described data as symbols representing the properties of experience. Information was defined as data that has been processed so that it is useful and is contained in descriptions. Knowledge represented answers to how-to questions and is contained in instructions. Understanding answers the why questions and is contained in explanations. Finally, wisdom concerns the value of outcomes; he termed this effectiveness, doing the right thing. Ackoff notes that five types of learning represent a hierarchy of value, with data having the least and wisdom the most.

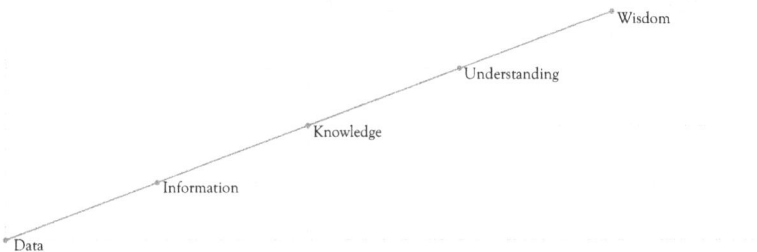

Wisdom

Understanding

Knowledge

Information

Data

Figure 4.1 Ackoff's system learning stages

Systems theorist have noted the relationships between these learning levels. To move from data to information requires that a relationship be established between the learner and what is to be learned. To move from information to knowledge necessitates that the learner see the patterns inherent in the information collected. To progress from knowledge to understanding, the learner must see the principles outside the system that provide the foundation upon which the patterns within the system operate. Finally, the progression from understanding to wisdom, the learner must see the natural laws from which the principles flow. As Ackoff notes, "The production of wisdom ... is a function primarily of ethics and aesthetics because it involves the conscious insertion of values into human decision making and evaluation of its outcomes."

Given the seven levels of moral development discovered by Kohlberg, I would posit that there are two additional stages of learning, creating a seven-stage process for systems thinking. This reformulated progression would be as follows: data, information, knowledge, **system**, understanding, wisdom, and **unity**. The modified relationships between these learning levels would consist of: object, relationships, pattern, **context**, principle, law, and **source**.

Systemic Leverage Points

> *When a person invests all her psychic energy into an interaction—whether it is with another person, a boat, a mountain, or a piece of music—she in effect becomes part of a system of action greater than what the individual self had been before. This system takes its form from the rules of the activity; its energy comes from the person's attention. But it is a real system—subjectively as real as being part of a family, a corporation, or a team—and the self that is part of it expands its boundaries and becomes more complex.*
>
> —Mihaly Csikszentmihalyi

In order to make effective change in any system, it would be wise to utilize leverage points, places within a complex system where a shift in one component can create big change in the entire system (Meadows, *Leverage Points: Places to Intervene in a System*, Sustainability Institute, 1999). In a list of places to intervene in a system (including locations such as the goals of system and the rules of the system), the second most effective location is one's mindset, their perspective. The first is the power to transcend paradigms, to go beyond one's mindset. Thus, if we wish to experience a more ideal interaction within our contextual system, we should focus on expanding our perspective, or perhaps even transcending it.

Philosophy

Plato

> *Philosophy begins with wonder.*
>
> —Plato

While philosophical theories have already been addressed in terms of normative ethical theories, the philosophy of Plato can best be understood as a descriptive account of how one can interact with their environment in an ideal manner. He is an exemplar. Plato can best be understood as one who actually developed an experiential understanding of how one goes about living a good life. He accomplished this by putting his philosophic theory of virtue ethics into practice.

Plato and other Greek philosophers made the same determination we did in asking why a person engages in any behavior. Ultimately, the intention is to promote your own happiness, to have a good experience of life. Your intention is your meaning. Intention is one of the most important concepts to truly understand. This is the Greek philosophical concept of *telos*, meaning purpose or intention, where you set your aim in life. Choose wisely. If you seek the Good via wisdom, your intention is to interact with the world in an ideal way.

These philosophers used the concept of *telos* to describe what you are aiming for. They analogized this to the aiming of a bow and arrow at a particular target. Your *telos* is your intention, where your bow is aimed. While doing so, a philosopher would advise you to do your best but to not be attached to the outcome, as any number of factors from wind to noise could affect whether or not your well-aimed shot actually hits the target at which you are aiming. It is important to realize how much more enjoyable life is if you focus your attention and intention on things you can control. For example, you can never completely control the outcome of any competitive event that you enter. But you can control how you choose to prepare for and participate in that competitive event. In other words, you control your intentions and actions, but not the consequences that naturally follow.

To understand the philosophical approach is to grasp that philosophers were intent on determining the natural laws, and the principles that describe them, that should be obeyed in order to live the best life possible. That's a pretty ambitious aim. The manner in which philosophers accomplished this is embedded in the meaning of the term "philosopher." It means lover of wisdom. Perhaps the ideal example of any philosopher to have ever lived is Plato.

Plato was the founder of the modern-day academic University; he founded the Academy for research and learning in 380 BC. As Alfred North Whitehead famously quipped, "The safest general characterization of the European philosophical tradition is that it consists of a series of footnotes to Plato." (Process and Reality, Free Press 1979, 39). Think for yourself: if you determine that there was a very wise individual who explained how to go about acquiring wisdom, which is the equivalent of enjoying your life experience, would you not give his ideas your attention? Plato has given each of us the blueprint for a happy, flourishing life, and we shall turn to it next.

Plato's Cave

> *Wisdom is the integration of moral imagination (the good), systems understanding (the true), and aesthetic sensibility (the beautiful) into decisions, (and) actions ... in the service of a better world. Moral imagination is the ability to see the ethical issues embedded in ... decisions, or what philosophers have long called "the good." Moral imagination has been linked to systems understanding which means a reasonably accurate perspective on the "system as a whole," or what we can call "the true." The third element of wisdom is aesthetic sensibility, or the ability to appreciate the design and aesthetic ... that is, what philosophers call "the beautiful."*
>
> —Donna Hicks and Sandra Waddock

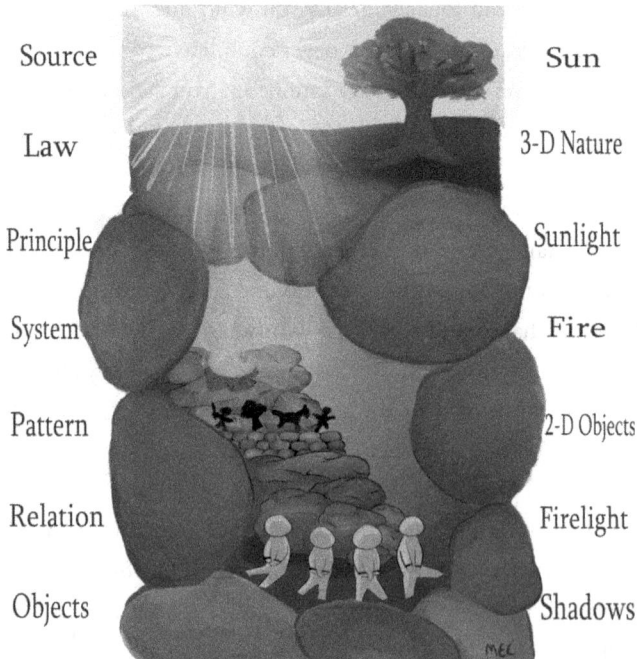

Figure 4.2 Plato's cave (illustrated by my daughter, Mary Chumney)

This remarkable allegory describes prisoners who are chained with their back to a fire that is both behind them and higher up (Figure 4.2). These chains only allow the prisoners to perceive the world that is directly in front of them, and they have been chained since childhood. Between the fire and prisoners, behind a raised platform, people carry flat, two-dimensional objects atop sticks above them; the light from the fire hits these objects and shadows are cast upon the cave wall that is directly in front of the prisoners. The prisoners only view the shadows on the wall and hear the noises made by those carrying the objects, believing these to be the ultimate reality.

To truly understand Plato's cave, you should imagine that you are the main character in the allegory and that you, along with the rest of humanity, are chained within a cave so that you can only look in one direction, forward to a blank wall. From this perspective, the only knowledge you and your fellow human beings have of reality is that of shadows moving about in front of you and the sound they seem to produce. Your fellow human beings use words to describe different relationships among these shadows, motivated by their sense of wonder. This constitutes your entire context, the world you experience, to the best of your knowledge.

Now, suppose you break free from your chains and are able to turn around and look, for the first time in your life, behind you. To your astonishment, you are initially blinded by a bright fire high above you. As your vision grows accustomed to the light, you are eventually able to see that the fire's light hits flat objects, shapes of natural objects, prior to reaching the perspective you and the rest of humanity initially possessed, when you were chained and looking ahead at the cave wall. Thus, your prior knowledge of your world was created originally by the fire burning high above you; the light of this fire then hit objects that were positioned between the fire and your initial chained position, and this process resulted in the shadows cast on the wall. Your knowledge has grown to encompass the fact that the two-dimensional objects casting the shadows are more real than the shadows they cast.

Examining those more real objects that create the shadows, with the help of the source fire that allows you to see anything at all in that cave via its light, you notice that they are being held by other human beings and that the noises you heard earlier when chained are created by these people and the noise echoes off the cave wall before being perceived by your sense of hearing. So your entire experience of reality before you broke free of your chains was created by other human beings, who were responsible for the two-dimensional objects being placed there, along with the words used by the chained human beings to describe them. But keep in mind that there would be no shadows without the originating fire and its light that shone upon those objects.

Having obtained greater knowledge of how your life experience is created, you notice another source of light whose source lies higher up and beyond the fire, that to this point has been the original source of the world you've come to know. There is a faint light you are able to perceive that when followed up a rough and steep ascent, leads to the mouth of the cave, which you have inhabited your entire life to this point.

Exiting the cave, you are blinded by a light source greater than any you could have ever imagined within the confines of the cave, just as you were blinded earlier when you first saw the fire. As you begin to walk in the natural setting outside the cave, you are unable to raise your gaze to perceive the source of this unimaginable bright light. So you understand your new surroundings by degrees. First, you see only shadows, then reflections of human beings and natural objects in water, and later the human beings and natural objects themselves. At this point, you have gone way beyond your initial knowledge of how things work. You have come to know that the flat shapes that were the more real source of the shadow you mistook for reality, were themselves pale imitations of these more real three-dimensional objects found in nature. Eventually, you are able to see these natural objects by the light of the moon, which is, of course, simply reflecting the light of the sun. Finally, you are able to directly gaze upon the true source of all living things on the planet, the sun. Furthermore, just as the fire was the source of what you perceived in the cave, with its light striking objects and casting shadows, the sun is the ultimate source of everything perceived both inside and outside the cave, and its sunlight strikes the natural objects and bounces into your eyes, allowing you to perceive the external natural world.

Upon reflection, one can see that there are seven distinct stages experienced by the human being as they embark upon a journey to exit the cave. These stages are reflected in Figure 4.2. The first experiential level consists of the shadows on the cave wall. The second stage is signified by the light from the fire that shines upon the objects that creates the shadows in the first stage. The third level of experience consists of the flat, two-dimensional objects being carried by other human beings within the cave, whose shadows the chained humans mistake for reality. The fourth stage is the fire, which is the original source of all that is experienced within the cave. The fifth level occurs when the sunlight is first seen in the cave and it leads to the mouth where one can exit. The sixth stage consists of experiencing the natural three-dimensional objects that exist in the world outside the cave by the light of the moon (which is, of course, the light of the sun reflected off of the moon). It should be noted that this stage is the first time a transcendental object, one beyond the world, is utilized to clearly see the natural objects that surround you. The final level of experience is the sun itself, the ultimate source of all life that exists both outside and within the cave.

Table 4.4 Seven stages of Plato's cave

Cave
Shadows
Firelight
2D Objects
Fire
Sunlight
Nature
Sun

This remarkable allegory explains the journey each of us can choose to embark upon. It is describing a level of personal growth we can each attain by wondering about the Truth and intending toward it. When asked about the most efficient path to achieve this level of knowledge, the answer provided by Plato was by way of the virtues.

Virtue

All the gold which is under or upon the earth is not enough to give in exchange for virtue.

—Plato

What Plato realized was that the transcendent nature of our context is moral and experienced most efficiently via practice of the virtues. Plato enumerated precisely four virtues that were both necessary and sufficient for any human being to experience a happy and flourishing life. In his own words: "Wisdom is the leader: next follows moderation; and from the union of these two with courage spring justice." This indicates that the path toward wisdom is of primary importance, along with the proper application, via attention and intention, of your reasoning mind. If you are then able to control your desires (moderation) and display persistence (courage) over fear in this pursuit, fairness (justice) will be manifest in your actions. Thus, the virtues put forth by Plato were: wisdom, courage, moderation, and justice.

Plato posited these four cardinal virtues that were considered to be both *necessary* and *sufficient* for one to experience a flourishing life. Before proceeding further, let's make sure we understand the meaning of those two words. Necessary means that in order to experience a flourishing life, it is required that one understand and practice the four virtues. Additionally, and of utmost importance, is the fact that these four virtues were sufficient, meaning that the understanding and practice of these virtues is **all** that is required for one to experience a flourishing life.

Transcendentals

> *The Good, the True, and the Beautiful are effectively united in the supreme creative principle, at once commanding moral affirmation, intellectual allegiance, and aesthetic surrender. As the most accessible of the Forms, visible in part even to the physical eye, Beauty opens up human awareness to the existence of the other Forms, drawing the philosopher toward the beatific vision and knowledge of the True and the Good. Hence Plato suggested that the highest philosophical vision is possible only to one with the temperament of a lover. The philosopher must permit himself to be inwardly grasped by ... that universal passion.*
>
> —Richard Tarnas

As alluded to in Chapter 1, Plato described the true nature of the world via three perspectives: the Good, the True, and the Beautiful. The Good is your ideal perspective from which you choose to view the world. The Beautiful can be construed as your ideal emotional perception of experiences within your context. The True is your ideal understanding of your context.

Tarnas' beautiful passage shown earlier is quite insightful. The first concept to take note of is that of "vision." This can be analogized to the human eye. Externally, we use our eyes to view our external context. Internally, we have inner "vision" that can be directed via our attention toward innumerable mental concepts. Most of us waste this most precious commodity by allowing our thoughts to wander from one negative concept to another, with the result being that we actually feel stress in whatever present moment we find ourselves in.

What Plato did was direct his attention inward toward the independently existing Idea of Beauty, which he found to be within himself. As he directed his vision toward Beauty, he perceived the True and the Good by accessing knowledge of them. By each of these ideas, Plato means that we are drawn to them in all of our endeavors, not in some limited context. They are universally applicable concepts that we are able to perceive in each of our interactions with our context, if we choose to see it.

Beauty is what draws out the emotion of love from within us toward some (usually external) entity. Beauty is most easily understood because most of us have experienced this in the physical world via visual perception. This can obviously be found in a variety of examples: the human form, a natural setting, and the mathematical underpinnings of the universe. This sense perception need not be visual, of course. One often finds beauty in song (I'd recommend Neil Young); the rhythm, beat, harmony, and metric of time interact with insightful lyrics and our interaction with those components has the power to affect our feelings, thoughts, and senses significantly.

By focusing on the process by which you are drawn toward Beauty, you can come to understand this concept of "Vision." Vision is your ability to direct the focus of your attention. It is a choice. By choosing to focus your attention on the experience of beauty in the material realm, one exercises the muscle of reason and increase the openness necessary to experience the Idea of Beauty, which transcends any particular expression of it in the material world. This is the alternate form of vision, one which is directed toward the principal ideas that can be made manifest in the material realm. Once vision is directed in this direction and connection is made, one can then turn their vision toward their conscious action and make it manifest. The degree to which you choose to limit the expansion of your inner vision in order to experience (and perhaps express) principal ideas is the extent to which you limit your power.

Plato notes that wisdom resulted from a "study of the whole order of things." The "whole order of things" can be understood most accurately as "context." And this approach is modern systems thinking from the mind of Plato. Notice that Plato is equating systems thinking as a critical aspect in determining the principles necessary to properly pursue wisdom. The "divine elements" can be understood as a level beyond knowledge, one of understanding, whereby principles, natural laws, are encountered (the sunlight that leads to the mouth of the cave and beyond).

Conscience

> *I decide on the basis of conscience. A genuine leader doesn't reflect consensus, he builds consensus.*
>
> —Martin Luther King, Jr.

Life is exactly as meaningful as you choose to make it. The simpler you make something, the more understandable it can become, depending on the focus of one's attention toward the words that are spoken. Once you come to value words and concepts over material acquisitions, you have begun to think for yourself. You now have general control over the instinctual fears and desires of the body, you've broken free of the chains in Plato's cave, and engaged reason in order to direct your attentive thoughts toward the beliefs you've been taught, which create the concepts that frame the way you perceive the world.

From a deeper perspective, you come to realize that you can utilize the gift of reason to discern both the nature of yourself and the truth of your context. The journey to understand both leads to the same place, where they intersect: consciousness, your perception of both yourself and the world. These two balance out: they are the yin and the yang. This is a universal symbol, signifying the balance inherent in all things conceptual or material. From a greater perspective, you realize they are both a component of the same thing.

The journey of reason proportionally corresponds to your experience of the present moment. The humans chained in Plato's cave represent reason, our ability to discern right from wrong, good from bad. We know this because we intuit the good from our conscience. The moon represents your conscience in Plato's allegory, its reflected light being sufficient to allow your vision of the principal ideas of nature, most concisely understood as the virtues. Beyond your conscience lies its source, consciousness, the ocean of which you and I are a part. This is the beautiful sun in Plato's allegory.

In Plato's cave allegory, the cave in its entirety represents you and I as systemic human beings composed of a body, a mind, and a heart. This is where you relate to the world in a less physically selfish way and more as an ideal human being, one who is transcendent.

Wisdom is living life in accord with our conscience. Philosophers at their original source were known as lovers of wisdom. Wisdom is the realization that you utilize the virtues to align your body, mind, and heart with your conscience and experience a flourishing life.

Love of Beauty

Wisdom is a practice that reflects the developmental process by which individuals increase in self-knowledge, self-integration, nonattachment, self-transcendence, and compassion, as well as a deeper understanding of life. This practice involves better self-regulation and ethical choices, resulting in greater good for oneself and others.
  —Richard Hawley Trowbridge and Michel Ferrari

Discussing the experience of love, Plato suggests in his writings that there are six stages that one must progress in order to experience the ideal form of love. The first stage is love of the physical body of a beautiful person. At the second stage, one realizes that beauty is similar in all persons, and we love all beautiful bodies. The third stage occurs when one loves the inner aspects of a person, their mind, to a greater degree than the beauty of their body. At the fourth stage, we see beauty in manmade institutions that were created by beautiful minds. The fifth stage is the love of philosophic ideas. The sixth and final stage is love of the form of beauty itself, the form from which all beautiful things experienced participate.

Soul

Subjective experience is not just one of the dimensions of life, it *is* life itself.

—Mihaly Csikszentmihaly

Plato used the concept of the Good to describe the true nature of our essence. In modern terms, this could be understood as consciousness. The soul was seen as who you really were, the identity that you discovered if you successfully embarked upon the journey to "Know Thyself." To speak the Truth to humanity who shared the same point in space and time with him, he chooses another allegory.

Plato used the analogy of a chariot being pulled through the air by two flying horses to illustrate the tripartite nature of the soul. One horse was noble and spirited, representing our heart, the nature of which is to intend toward the moral Good if so directed. The second horse was wild and stubborn, representing our bodily feelings away from those things that we fear and toward those things that we desire. The charioteer represents the reasoning mind that must direct both the body and the heart toward the higher Good with great effort. This great effort can be understood as the practical application of the virtues. The higher perspective of the transcendent soul is represented by the entire interrelated system. This proper direction is toward transcendence. If one uses reason appropriately, they can control their desires and overcome their innate fear while properly pursuing the good intentions of the heart. Plato is saying that the essence of who you and I are, our soul, consists of three components: the body, the mind, and the heart. We are a system.

Table 4.5 Components of Plato's chariot

Plato's Chariot	Soul System
Dark Horse	Body
White Horse	Heart
Charioteer	Mind
Chariot System	Soul

The Descriptive Business Ethics Triad

The pursuit of the truth is the scientific and technological function of societies. It consists of encouraging and facilitating the production of the information, knowledge, and understanding required by individuals to select the most efficient means available and to develop means that are increasingly efficient.

—Russell Ackoff

Just as business ethics generally and normative business ethics more specifically were seen in relationship to each other via a triangle, descriptive business ethics theories have their own relational triad (Figure 4.3). We have already seen that the perspectives of "you" and "deontology" are aligned. The descriptive business ethics theory that builds on these is psychology. Similarly, "business" and "utilitarianism" are aligned, and the descriptive theory that best describes these is systems theory. Finally, we have seen that "ethics" and "virtue" are aligned; the descriptive theory that supports them is the philosophy of Plato.

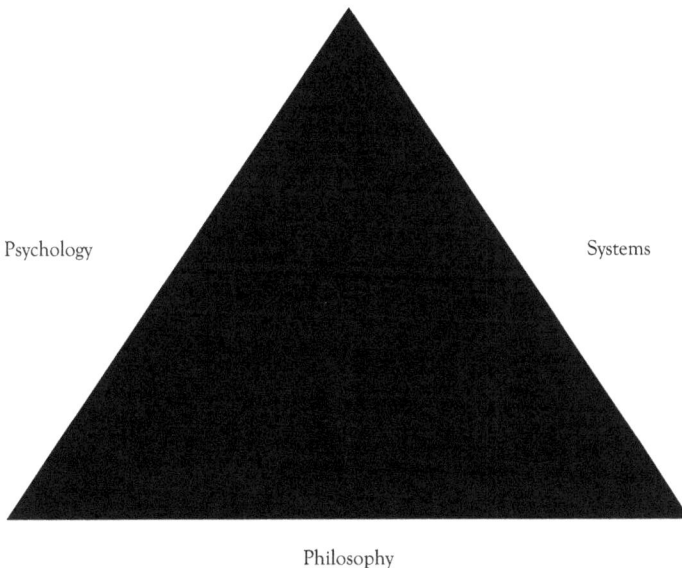

Psychology   Systems

Philosophy

Figure 4.3 The descriptive business ethics triad

What follows is a transcendent approach to business ethics. What this means is that the ideas it contains both unify and supersede the three primary approaches to understanding and teaching business ethics: deontology, utilitarianism, and virtue ethics. Beyond these normative theories of how to ideally interact with the world, one should apply descriptive theories to understand that same interaction. Psychology applies to you, systems theory applies to the world, and philosophy applies to the interaction between the internal and external components of the system.

CHAPTER 5

Conscious Business Ethics

Meaning

The knowledge of how to control consciousness must be reformulated every time the cultural context changes. The wisdom of the mystics, of the Sufi, of the great yogis, or of the Zen masters might have been excellent in their own time—and might still be the best, if we lived in those times and in those cultures. But when transplanted to contemporary California those systems lose quite a bit of their original power. They contain elements that are specific to their original contexts, and … the path to freedom gets overgrown by brambles of meaningless mumbo jumbo. Ritual form wins over substance …

— Mihaly Csikszentmihalyi

We now have a sufficient comprehension of business ethics to present the CBE model, which I refer to as the Game of Life. Recall our prior discussion of the business ethics triad, consisting of you, business, and ethics. CBE can be presented as follows: You are conscious, your context is business, and ethics is how you choose to interact with the business system in an ideal manner (Figure 5.1). CBE integrates the fields of each normative and descriptive approach to business ethics and simplifies it into a simple symbol that is able to be understood by anyone who desires to learn. Here, in Table 5.1, are the transdisciplinary relationships covered so far in terms of descriptive business ethics.

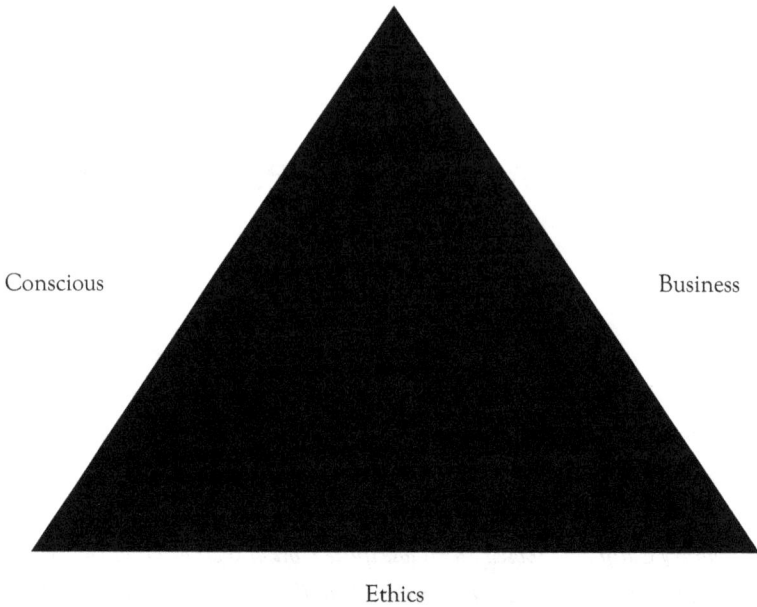

Conscious   Business

Ethics

Figure 5.1 The conscious business ethics triad

Table 5.1 Relationship between psychology, systems, and philosophy

Psychology	Systems	Philosophy
Fear	Data	Shadows
Attention	Information	Firelight
Belief Conformity	Knowledge	2D Objects
Societal Conformity	System	Fire
Unifying Principles	Understanding	Sunlight
Conscience	Wisdom	Nature/Moon
Transcendence	Truth	Sun

Consciousness is the core essence of our life experience, which Plato called the soul. There are three primary components that emanate from this soul: body, mind, and heart, the interaction of which creates the action one takes in the physical world. In the game of life, the best outcome is achieved by operating each of these components in as ideal a manner as possible. Plato called such ideal operations virtues, thus creating the foundational philosophic source of our modern approach to virtue ethics.

Plato had inscribed the following phrase above the entrance to his Academy, the first University in the Western World: "Let none ignorant of geometry enter here." My understanding of the severity of this statement is that geometry reveals the relationship between the various components of one's life, and one must learn to use them properly in order to create a good experience. To that end, I correlated the findings of three great minds from three different perspectives. The result is a unifying structure that can be utilized to understand your life experience and how to use the leverage point of your perspective to intend toward being your idea of an ideal human being.

My intention with this model is to demonstrate, in the simplest manner possible, the relationship between the most critical components of your life in order to provide you the power to create as good an experience as possible for yourself and others. From the perspective of philosophy, CBE makes business ethics functional by simply revealing the relationship between what is of most fundamental import in one's life. From the perspective of science, CBE operationalizes the findings of psychology, systems thinking, and philosophy. From the perspective of business, CBE provides a blueprint each of us can practically apply to our own lives in order to both have a better experience and create a better culture within that context.

CBE is a modern practical approach to business ethics. The simplest way to comprehend this approach is to treat the CBE symbol as a geometric representation of the Game of Life, and CBE shows you how to best play this game so that you win. Each of the most important components that need to be utilized to accomplish this goal will be explained and interrelated within a systemic view. As the earlier discussion of philosophy and science makes clear, you win the game of life by living a good life, by taking good actions, and having a good life experience.

To accomplish this seemingly extraordinary feat, there are three simple words that I would encourage you to keep in mind, and their inspiration originates from the time of Socrates: Think for Yourself. These are the three words I can imagine are whispered in the prisoner's ear prior to his ascension out of the cave. This is the simple instruction given to sincere individuals who wish to truly understand the Truth of themselves and how they should play the game of life. Table 5.2 lists the stages one encounters if they heed this advice.

Table 5.2 Stages of conscious business ethics

CBE
Perception
Attention
Retention
Perspective
Understanding
Conscience
Transcendence
Central "I"

The Game of Life

At this point, almost all the components needed to understand how consciousness can be controlled are in place. We have seen that experience depends on the way we invest psychic energy—on the structure of attention. This, in turn, is related to goals and intentions. These processes are connected to each other by the self, or the dynamic mental representation we have of the entire system of our goals. These are the pieces that must be maneuvered if we wish to improve things.

—Mihaly Csikszentmihalyi

The CBE symbol is a geometric representation of the game of life (Figure 5.2). It can most easily be understood as an information system within which you choose how to process the data that you experience in your life. It demonstrates in as simple a manner as possible, the interrelationship of each critical components necessary for accomplishing the goal of living a good life.

Begin by looking at the three vertices of the triangle, starting on the lower left and going clockwise. This is a model of how you see the world. Stated differently, it's about the perspective you choose, from which you perceive your context. With this in mind, we will examine how to live a good life from the inside out.

YOU are the center of your conscious life experience. This is represented by the Φ sign located in the very center of the model. Notice that it is located at the intersection of your conscious experience. Be aware also

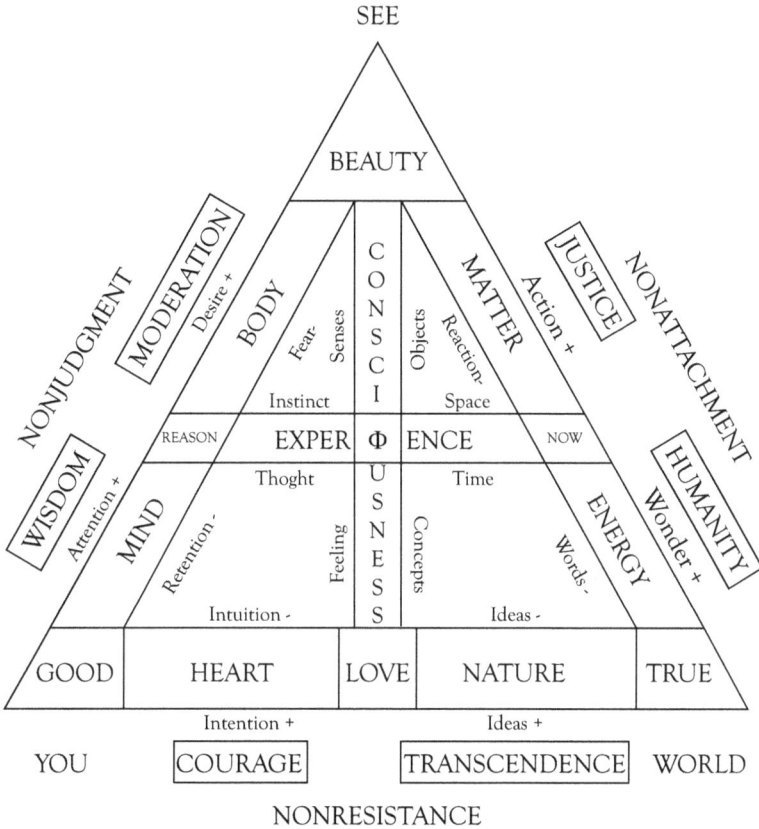

Figure 5.2 The game of life

of the balance demonstrated at this point where YOU are located. From this balanced center point, realize that there are two sides to everything: an inside and an outside. The left side of the diagram is the inner YOU experience and the right side is the outer YOU experience.

Focusing on the left side of the equation, there are three components that comprise your inner experience. Your body, your mind, and your heart. Each of these are balanced by your outer experience of matter, energy, and nature. Given that you are a living system, each of your inner components interacts with its outer counterpart. The nature of this interaction is found on the inner and outer line of consciousness. Your body interacts with matter by sensing objects on this physical level. Your mind interacts with energy by thinking about concepts on this mental level. Finally, your heart interacts with nature by feeling. Think about this for yourself: the only conscious experience you can have at any point in space and time is what you sense with your body, think with your mind, or feel with your heart.

Developing a greater understanding of how these three primary internal components function, we examine their subcomponents. Your body operates on the basis of instinct (habit), which is informed by fear (pain) and desire (pleasure). Consider the functions your body performs without any attention from your mind: breathing, regulating hormone levels, and digesting the food you eat, to name just a few. These are instinctual in nature. Similarly, there are many habits that you engage in throughout your daily routine. These are unconscious decisions being made at the physical level of your body. Thus, your body tends to function on autopilot without much input from your reasoning mind.

The primary motivators of your bodily actions can most simply be understood as fear and desire. Fear is what draws you away from an external object that you experience. Desire is what draws you toward the same. Alternatively, you could conceive of these primary motivators of your body as pain and pleasure.

Your mind functions by thinking on the basis of its attention and retention (beliefs). Your attention can be thought of as your most valuable asset. It is where you consciously choose to focus the power of your mind to develop knowledge. The only way you can come to know what you don't know is to focus your attention on those things. Once you focus your attention on an object, it becomes data for your mind to retain certain beliefs about that object, as well as its relationship to all other known objects.

Your heart functions by feeling on the basis of intention and intuition. The intention that you bring to bear in your life is incredibly important. Though you have many intentions at various times, this is referring to the primary intention with which you choose to live your life. This is what gives your life meaning and determines what you value in your life experience. Furthermore, the intention that guides your life will carry your attention along with it, so that it will only be able to focus the mind's perceptive ability within the context that your intention carries you. The intuition of natural principles is what allows for understanding of a relationship to a system greater than yourself.

Turning to the outside, your body interacts with objects in matter based on action taken in the physical world and the reaction perceived in response. Action is a result of a conscious decision you make to interact with other human beings or objects in the physical world. Based on those actions you choose to take, there will necessarily be a reaction from your external context. This is what you perceive as data, the objects that you perceive via the attention focused by your mind.

On the energetic level, your mind interacts with concepts based on words and wonder. Words are the representation of our mental concepts. They segment the wholeness of our experience into fragments that our mind is able to retain. They operate at a conceptual level to segment reality into acceptable standards at the societal level. Wonder is the energy that motivates one's mind to focus its attention on particular objects or concepts. As Plato said, "Philosophy begins with wonder." One should wonder about the nature of things (themselves, objects, and concepts included).

Your heart interacts with nature based on your understanding of ideas and ideals. Ideas represent those principles that reflect the universal laws upon which the universe (and consequently, your world) operates. Ideals represent the inherent nature of the greater life system of which we are a part. As has been noted throughout the text, each philosophic and scientific approach to living a good, flourishing life has pointed toward the ideal. Thus, from a philosophic and scientific perspective, if it is your intention to experience a good life, you are aspiring toward an ideal.

Focusing once again on the CBE symbol and the horizontal line of experience, every single experience you ever have takes place now, at a particular point in space and time. The quality of that experience is most directly determined by whether or not you use reason appropriately. Using reason you can wonder about the words used to conceptualize your experience right now, and intend toward a good life. Generally speaking, you can accomplish this goal by working on becoming your ideal idea of a good human being.

Turning once again to the CBE symbol, we should note that an ideal life is one that experiences the aforementioned transcendentals. The beautiful can best be understood as the ideal perception. The true is the ideal context. The good is the ideal perspective.

Recalling the method revealed by Plato and validated by modern psychologists, the relationship of the virtues to these various life components must be understood. As Heraclitus so eloquently observed, "Character is destiny." Who you really are determines what your experience of life will be. Thus, practicing the six virtues we've explored are both **necessary** and **sufficient** to experience an ideal life. Notice that each of these virtues is contained within each of the six major components of your life experience. One must practice moderation in order to properly make decisions without being overcome by the fears and desires of the body. In order to interact most effectively with your external environment, the virtue of justice, fairness, should be the guide of your actions. Your mind with its attention and retention should be guided by the ideal of wisdom. On the energetic level, humanity should be the virtue that guides both the words you utilize to conceptualize your world and the wonder that motivates your reasoning mind to ultimately seek the Truth. Courage, perseverance, should guide the intention of your heart, regardless of the societal norms within which you find yourself. Finally, you should practice transcendence toward the ideal ideas of nature.

The School of Life

The object of education is to teach us to love what is beautiful.

—Plato

Based on both the normative and descriptive approaches to business ethics, I would posit to you that the proper perspective to take on life is that it is a school, a university, literally, as it represents the entire Universe that comprises your world. Each context you experience (business, family, social, etc.) is one of the ongoing courses. The daily experience you have within each of these contexts is your class lesson. With each class lesson (experience) in each of these courses, you have a choice as to how you interact with the system. From Kohlberg's perspective, you either behave at a selfish physical level (preconventional), follow the prevailing norms (conventional), or strive toward the ideal (postconventional). At the two extremes, you can either base your choice on fear or you can base your choice on love. Of course, there exist various options in between, but these are beginning and end points for the basis on which you choose (from least ideal to most ideal) to interact with the class lessons (experience) within each course (context) that you encounter during your total life experience (University).

We can utilize Plato's original allegory of the cave to better understand the seven components of the School of Life within the CBE approach. There are seven distinct stages that you (as the character in the story) pass through. Each of those stages bring you closer to an understanding of the proper relationship among all things, of Truth.

You should be cognizant of the fact that the allegory of Plato's cave illustrates the effect of a proper education on human nature. What is the education he refers to? The meaning of education is moral development, and education in this university is the meaning of life. It is Plato's intention to educate your soul on how to live a good life. As we analyze the stages one goes through, we now understand that the application of the virtues to one's life is the most efficient way to progress through these stages.

Note that each stage contains an element of truth, but the higher your progress, the closer you come to the True, an understanding of how things really work. You have a certain level of knowledge, but you are able, via the proper application of reason, to expand beyond that current level (you don't know what you don't know). So this search for Truth is the same as the search for Self, the same as gaining a better understanding of the proper relationship among all things, reality.

The first stage is represented by the shadows on the wall. I term this stage perception. It is the original orientation we have, and its limited context informs our decision regarding what actions to take. The second stage is represented by the fire light that permits the shadows to be seen. I call this stage attention. The third stage is represented by the objects held by other human beings that are flat and resemble natural objects. This stage can be understood as belief, or retention. You consider yourself as identifying with those other human beings who share beliefs similar to yours. The fourth stage is represented by the burning fire that is the originating source of everything within the cave. This stage is representative of the sum total of all you have retained using your attention and beliefs to create your conscious experience of reality. It can best be comprehended as your mind set, your perspective. At this point you realize that there are various beliefs held by varied human beings that comprise humanity, and that those societies created by humanity must incorporate the view of the majority. These can best be understood as societal norms.

The real change occurs when one moves beyond the first four stages. The fifth stage is represented by sunlight emanating from the Sun, which leads to the mouth of the cave. This is the level of Understanding. It is at this point that one first has a form of intuition or insight that something greater than oneself exists. Hence the opening to a greater perspective, a greater understanding of what is more true, more real. This is the first stage beyond the contextual system of societal norms. The sixth stage is represented by nature and the living beings found outside the cave as seen by the light of the moon. I term this level of development wisdom. At this level, one understands the proper relationship among all things, and is experiencing a good life by acting in accordance with their conscience. Conscience is symbolized by the moon, as it reflects the light of the source, the Sun. The seventh stage is represented by the Sun. This is the True context, the Good perspective, and the Beautiful perception. It is the ultimate source of all that is experienced, since its light provides the energy that sustains all life on Earth.

It's all reflections: the Source, Life, shines its light onto your mindset, your perspective, which shines its light (attention) through its retained beliefs onto the exterior objects and mental concepts that it experiences as objects. Looking at it the other way, we are all part of greater living systems that can be found both within us and without. Furthermore, there's a moral component to life and life is a process of learning and growing via experience.

Plato notes that the fastest way to exit the cave, to pass through the various stages in the school of life, is to practice the virtues. As you embark on this journey, keep in mind that there are stages you have yet to encounter, so there are experiences and things that you don't know you don't know. You're looking at shadows and believing them to be the source of who you are. The system that comprises the human soul can best be effectively understood as a system composed of body, mind, and heart, which perceive the world through senses, thoughts, and feelings.

You are greater than you believe yourself to be. Don't get subsumed into playing the role of who you presently believe yourself to be. You don't know what you don't know. Engage life so as to develop who you are into a more ideal human being and interact with the world in a more ideal way. Each experience you consciously encounter can best be understood as a life lesson, one that you can utilize to intentionally progress up these stages to begin practicing Plato's ideal of love instead of the material practice of fear.

Ideally, you should aim toward seeing the beauty in yourself and the world by making decision on the basis of love. Ideally, you should see the good in yourself and make decisions based on what is good both for yourself and others. Ideally, you should make decisions based on what is true both of yourself and of your world.

The Journey of Reason

The most concise description of the approach I believe to be the clearest way to examine the main facets of what happens in the mind, in a way that can be useful in the actual practice of everyday life, is "a phenomenological model of consciousness based on information theory." This representation of consciousness is phenomenological in that it deals directly with events—phenomena—as we experience and interpret them, rather than focusing on the anatomical structures, neurochemical processes, or unconscious purposes that make these events possible.

—Mihaly Csikszentmihalyi

The journey of reason can be understood as how one experiences life both internally and externally (Figure 5.3). Recall our earlier discussions of the business (you, business, and ethics), normative (deontology, utilitarianism, and virtue) and descriptive (psychology, systems, and philosophy) triads, as they inform this journey. Remember this is about how you see the world. The experience you have will be informed by the seven stages of moral development discovered by Kohlberg. The experience of your world will be informed by Ackoff's levels of systems. Finally how you see, how you interact with the world, will be informed by the philosophy of Plato and his six stages of love of beauty.

The journey of reason ultimately determines our experience of life. As reason embarks upon this journey, this power informs both our perspective and our perception. Thus, the proper focus of reason both alters the framework from which we observe the world and also the depth with which we perceive it. At the first stage, the power of reason focuses attention on the instinctual fear of the body, and consequently, perceives their

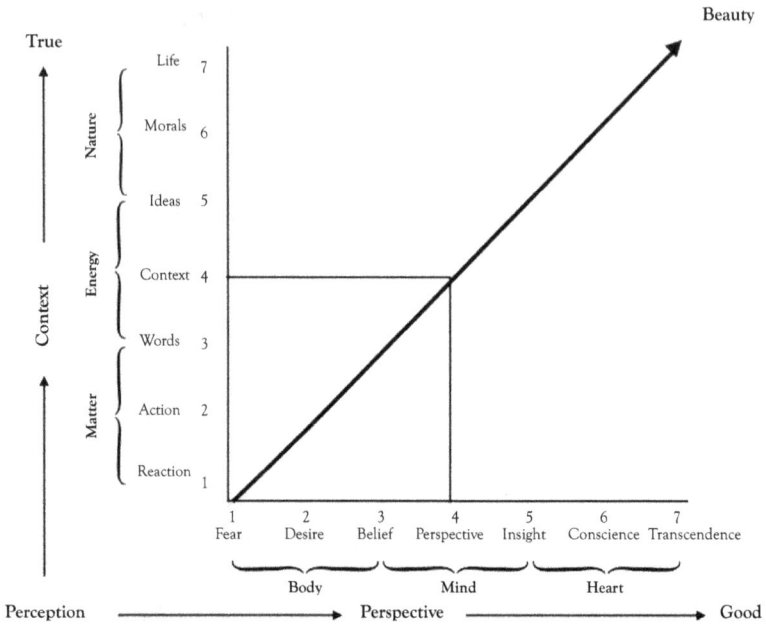

Figure 5.3 The journey of reason

world primarily focused on the reactions received when interacting with various people and objects during the present moment. At the second stage, reason filters attention toward instinctual desires and relates to the world with actions aimed toward this intention. At the third stage, reason focuses attention on the beliefs you retain and sees the patterns present in the words used to conceive the world. At the fourth stage, one develops reason to the point of perspective and sees the totality of the system within its present context. At the fifth stage, one has chosen to go beyond the normal system within which most of humanity operates. Here one utilizes the power of intuition to perceive the principles that form from eternal ideas. At the sixth stage, you are in alignment with your conscience; you perceive the laws from which nature flows, and you realize they are moral in nature. At the seventh stage, you transcend toward the ideals of unity with the transcendent living source of all things.

The six stages of love, as outlined by Plato, correspond with the perception of beauty, an ideal. The first stage is love of a single beautiful body, which correlates to the most basic act of perception. The next level is relation, which occurs when one notices the relationship between beauty and all bodies that partake of that form. The third level occurs when one goes beyond the physical level and experiences the love of a beautiful mind. At the fourth level, one sees beauty in the laws and institutions developed by those with beautiful minds. At the fifth stage, one loves the beauty of philosophic principles, such as the virtues, which are the basis of the beauty beheld in institutions. At stage six, one comes to love the ideal form of beauty itself, and comes to the realization that all those beautiful things experienced below this level are beautiful because of their connection to this ideal. The final (unstated) stage seven can be understood as Unity, the source of Beauty, Truth, and Good.

Table 5.3 reveals the remarkable relationships between Plato's Cave, Kohlberg's stages of moral development, and Plato's love of beauty as contained within the CBE model put forth in this text.

Table 5.3 Relationship between CBE, Plato's cave, Kohlberg's moral development, and Plato's love of beauty

CBE	Cave	Moral Development Level	Love of Beauty
Perception	Shadows	Fear	A Beautiful Body
Attention	Firelight	Attention	All Beautiful Bodies
Retention	2D Objects	Belief Conformity	Beautiful Minds
Knowledge	Fire	Societal Conformity	Beauty of Institutions
Understanding	Sunlight	Unifying Principles	Beautiful Principles
Wisdom	Nature	Conscience	Beauty Itself
Transcendence	Sun	Transcendence	Unity
Central "Φ"	Human Being/ Soul	Decision Maker	Beholder of Beauty

The Education of Self

Intelligence plus character—that is the goal of true education.
—Martin Luther King

One way to approach the CBE paradigm is to follow the frames through which one generally views the world within four developmental stages. What follows is an explanation of each linear component of the CBE model in the order of developmental attainment.

Physical

The first frame or lens is that of our material context, the visible, physical world. This is the realm within which we interact with other human beings or objects that are located within our natural and artificial environments. We interact with the physical realm via our actions, which can be seen from our perspective as a positive force; and we receive data from our physical environment from the reactions that we receive via the perception of our physical senses. These reactions can also be understood as the consequences, or outcomes, of our actions.

Plato views the physical context to be the shadows on the wall in the seminal cave allegory. It is also represented as Data, the first in the four frames of conscious experience. This is the most base and limited conscious experience we can have. To move beyond and experience the next level, we must first see the relationship between these external physical images that we perceive primarily via the visual sense of our eyesight. Critically, Plato made it clear in the cave allegory that these external objects that we interact with are merely a reflection of an object that is more real. So, in order to experience the higher level of conceptual experience, we must refocus our attention from its generally external focus and bring it to bear upon what the more real thing is that these engaging external objects are reflective of: our beliefs. This requires an internal focus of one's attention, that is, self reflection.

Virtue in Action

Within this self-imposed limited perceived physical context, the most effective way to interact with it is for your actions to be fair in general and kind toward your fellow human beings, as deep down at the "Φ" level, we all genuinely are the same. This is the simplest way I know how to express the two virtues that Plato and positive psychology put forth as the best way to act in order to experience the ideal idea of a good human being: justice and humanity.

The Body

The second frame or lens is that of your physical body. The senses of your body are the primary point of perception into your external physical context. Thus, the senses of the body inform our experience and therefore the perspective we come from when engaging the external physical context. Our body performs instinctual functions that are designed to keep us alive. The body also tends to function as a creature of habit, continuing to subconsciously follow a course of conduct until one makes a conscious choice to do otherwise. From our internal perspective, our body has two basic instinctual/habitual reactions to the data that passes through it. The first is for the body to withdraw from something in the external environment; this is fear. Conversely, the body is drawn toward external objects via one's desires. Plato views the perspective of the body to be the relational connection between the external objects that are reflections of the beliefs found in one's mind. It is also represented as information, the second of the frames of conscious experience. While a broader context and perspective is consciously experienced here, there are even greater possibilities. To get there we must demonstrate sufficient control of our bodily instincts and habits before we then intend the more challenging task of mastering our mind.

Virtues of the Body

Within the perspective of the body, focusing your reason to exercise moderation over your instinctual fears and desires will best position you toward the experience of a happy and fulfilling life.

The Mind

The mind is the source of two critical powers in terms of your conscious experience of life: beliefs and attention. Our beliefs consist of those conscious experiences we choose to retain in order to help inform us about future actions we should take within our context. Our attention is where we consciously choose to focus our thoughts at any particular point in space and time. Just as we interact with our body in external physical space, we interact with our mind within a conceptual context. The mind consciously perceives our context via thought, just as the body perceives our context via the physical senses, primarily vision. The primary function of the properly engaged mind is to discern what information should be paid attention to and retained in order to generate knowledge of one's context so that one can interact with it in a more ideal manner.

Conceptual

We experience the conceptual realm when we extend the relationships present between ourselves and external objects as well as the relationship between external objects themselves. This is what one generally calls knowledge. It is when one has effectively utilized their mind to understand the relationships within a particular conceptual context. In the conceptual realm, one exercises no direct physical interaction with the system components. Energy provides the foundation upon which modern understandings of physics are conceptually based. The concepts of words and wonder provide one's mind with the tools necessary to more positively interact conceptually with our context.

Perspective

The third level that provides a frame through which to view the meaning of your life is your perspective. This comprises the internal component of the mind and the external conceptual context upon which it focuses its attention and intention.

Virtues of the Mind

Within the perspective of the mind, focusing your attention and beliefs on the principles of wisdom will eventually allow you to turn your focus from a knowledge of life primarily focused externally on one's physical context, instead toward an understanding based on the principles that form the natural laws or algorithms that generate a good life. One should note that the virtue of wisdom is what extends to the conceptual level in order to provide insight into the transcendent principles.

The Heart

Just as we use our mind to interact within the conceptual context, we use our heart to interact with the Good, which is what provides us with the ability to experience life at any conscious level of experience. By properly focusing our intention on the Good, we are able to consciously experience a Good Life via the creative intuition we receive in the form of positive feelings that naturally flow from the Good source. This can be understood as the transcendent/moral realm, which is experienced via feelings and intuition. With the transcendent realm, we accurately experience natural feelings of a positive nature as their source is the Good.

Virtues of the Heart

Focusing your attention and intention on the transcendent/moral level will allow you to consciously experience the unconditional love that lies naturally beyond one's conceptual mind. Good feelings naturally arise when one has transcended the more limiting development frameworks for understanding the meaning of one's life. The primary method for achieving this transcendental experience is the genuine expression of gratitude toward the greater interrelated contextual system of which you and I are a part.

Nature

We interact with the realm of Nature via the feelings inherent in our heart. It requires a good intention and the focus of one's attention on the ideal ideas contained therein. When we access this intuitive creative connection to our Good source, we consciously experience the happy, flourishing, meaningful life that we all truly seek.

The Six Virtues

Mortal life cannot offer you anything better than justice and truth; that is, peace of mind in the conformity of your actions to the laws of reason, … remember always what the world-nature is and what your own nature is and that your nature is such a small fraction of so cast a whole. Then you will recognize that no man can hinder you from conforming each word and deed to that nature of which you are a part.

—Marcus Aerulius

The six virtues represent the principles of nature that one discovers as they develop their moral reasoning. As we have seen, each of the virtues gleaned from both philosophy and psychology can be assigned to a variable component on our Model of Life. Justice is the proper application of action in the material world. Moderation is the proper application of reason over your bodily instincts of fear and desire. Wisdom is the proper application of reason in order to determine your mind's perspective. Courage is the proper application of love toward self in order to develop resilience toward whatever experience life brings you. Humanity is the proper application of your words and wonder toward your fellow human beings in order to genuinely care for them as equals. Transcendence is the proper integration of one's intention and intuition with the transcendental ideal ideas. The lifelong journey toward each of these virtues is initiated with the faculty of reason.

Justice

Justice means minding one's own business and not meddling with other men's concern.

—Plato

Justice corresponds with the action variable that takes place within the material realm. It involves the ability to be fair and respect the rights of others, including their differences. Justice can most simply be thought of as fairness. The transition here can be thought of as the proper application of reason to transform egoism into fairness. Egoism or selfishness is the foundation upon which our actions are initially based. But through the use of reason, one can replace this behavior with justice, or fairness.

Moderation

Moderation is associated with the body component of the CBE model. Moderation is the ability to overcome instinctual desire and fears while remaining balanced. With the proper application of reason, these can be overcome. The key to proper control of one's fears and desires is to focus your attention on what you do have, as opposed to what you lack.

Wisdom

Wisdom is associated with the mind component of the CBE model. Wisdom is the equivalent of living in accordance with one's conscience. It can also be understood as the state of flow in positive psychology. It is the proper understanding of all relationships among all known things. Wisdom is the experience of living the principles on a daily basis; it is the by-product of practicing the virtues.

Humanity

Humanity is the virtue of caring for each and every one of your fellow human beings. You and any other randomly selected human are 99.99 percent more similar than you and any other randomly chosen entity in the universe. By definition (or the process of rounding up), we are the same within this context. When you care for someone, your interaction with them is markedly more remarkable. The goal in this variable would be to utilize reason properly in order to transform selfish interactions with humanity into caring interactions with humanity. As you might imagine, it consists of all human beings, those who are no longer with us in the present, and those who will be in the present long after us. As with justice or fairness, the virtue of humanity begins with actions that are egoistic or selfish. But this can be replaced with care, kindness, as one applies reason.

Stakeholders are an important concept for the virtue of humanity. This term from the business world refers to any entity who has a stake in a decision that you make. While most business students refer to stakeholders, one concept to help understand this virtue is this: a stakeholder is merely a placeholder for the human perspectives that lie beyond what we perceive as a stakeholder. Almost every objective entity we term as a stakeholder consists of a collection of human beings. By obfuscating this fact, we neglect to care for our fellow human beings.

In fact, this obfuscation of the human perspective lies at the root of why the education of business ethics generally fails to effectuate changes in behavior for those students taking the course. In order to effectuate change in the behavior of business ethics students, one must focus on the perspective of both the individual decision maker and that of the various stakeholders affected by the decision that is effectuated. You are not defined by a single attribute, so why are your stakeholders? They are just as deep and complex as you.

Courage

The virtue of courage correlates to the heart component in our model. Courage is the ability to overcome one's fears and possess strength in adversity. It is critical to overcome the base emotion motivating most human behavior: fear. Fear is the general foundational basis of our emotions. By employing reason effectively, one can overcome fear and replace it with a more ideal emotion such as love.

Transcendence

Transcendence can also be known as the True, Good, and Beautiful. It is the truth of knowing who you really are. This is the ultimate conclusion of the search to "Know Thyself." From this peaceful center, you are able to make good decisions regarding how to interact with the system you find yourself in.

The Three Laws

Nonresistance, nonjudgment, and nonattachment are the three aspects of true freedom and enlightened living.

—Eckhardt Tolle

The habitual practice of these six virtues will result in a transformation of the self. This change is what wisdom traditions from various cultures teach. Change can be understood as the process of learning by reason. The transformation of data into more valuable forms is a process of learning and change. As one goes deeper into the practice, one comes to experience Plato's three transcendental laws of nature: the True, the Good, and the Beautiful. The ultimate natural laws revealed by practicing the ideal of being a good human being are the three laws from which the six virtues flow. This results in a beautiful interaction with your world (and any of its contexts), a good perspective from which to view the world (and any of its contexts), and a true understanding of the world (and any of its contexts) that you inhabit. Simply put, you feel good, you think true, and you sense beauty. Recall that the stage of development that corresponds with the law is that of wisdom, being in alignment with your conscience.

Your conscience is signified by the moon in Plato's allegory, the first transcendent light source that allows you to see the natural principles of virtue. The only thing to experience beyond these laws is the one source, of which you and I are both part.

The experience of Truth leads to nonattachment. In the now moment, nonattachment allows one to detach themselves from all external objects and concepts of the world. This results from one realizing that it is only reasonable to focus one's efforts on those things one can absolutely control. All external experiences must be accepted and applied toward one's life-long education, the purpose of which is to obtain the perspective afforded when reason is applied toward wisdom.

The experience of Good translates into nonjudgment in the reason behind one's thoughts. Most of our thoughts constantly judge the world, our fellow human beings, their beliefs, and our selves. Nonjudgment requires one to refrain from passing judgment on any beliefs or actions one observes. This practice would mean that you realize that any action a fellow human being takes would be undertaken by you if: (1) if you were having the exact same conscious experience at the same point in space and time, and (2) you had experienced the exact same life as your fellow human being up to that point in space and time.

The experience of Truth leads to the practice of nonresistance in the relationship you have with your context, your world. Once you are able to realize that you are related to a greater living natural creative system, you should be able to comprehend that your best course of conduct is to not resist the uncontrollable events you experience. But rather, the ideal human being would seek to transform each undesired experience into a learning experience that can help one progress toward wisdom. Acceptance provides the highly sought-after peace of mind that allows you to make a good decision, without your judgment being clouded.

The third dimension of this model is anchored by the" 'I" at the center of your conscious experience. Viewing your experiences from this level has a dramatic effect on your conscious experience and the relationship between this and your perspective, perception, and context. Consistently engaging life at this level of understanding has the following effects. First, you understand what it means to practice nonjudgment because you realize that if you were in another person's shoes and possessed their body, mind, and heart, and had gone through each and every one of their experiences, you would act in exactly the same way. Within your perception of life, you realize that practicing nonresistance is the only reasonable path. Your perception of experiences will come and they will go; they do not define who you are. Regarding each present moment experience, one realizes that in order to remain free from the constantly changing external things you experience, it is imminently more sensible to practice nonattachment and not relate your emotional well-being to any external uncontrolled object or concept. In this way, you keep your power in order to interact more ideally with your context.

You

In theory there is no difference between theory and practice. In practice there is.

—Yogi Berra

Practice. The value of this entire text is fundamentally about that word. Not obviously, of course, but unless you actually comprehend the material contained in this text and then make the all-important decision to actually put them into practice, these words are meaningless. Words are miniature metaphors for meaning. It is the meaning behind the words of this text that have value. And their value can only be realized if they are put into practice.

To begin a practical approach to business ethics, we should realize that you (and I) can be viewed as a system that takes in data in order to manage the knowledge we've gained, so that we can experience a good life. The answer to how to most effectively process that data and transform it into more useful knowledge is provided originally by the philosophy of Plato, and more recently by the field of psychology and systems thinking.

Numerous human beings throughout this planet's history have thought deeply and practiced habitually what it means to be an ideal, happy, flourishing human being. This book has distilled the essence of all those various wisdom traditions across various cultures into a simple diagram that can fit on a T-shirt. Stated one way: if something so valuable were made so accessible, it should be worth pursuing.

The CBE model demonstrates that you ("Φ") are the exact center of your conscious experience in space and time with your state of consciousness depending on what you sense, think, and feel. You determine what you perceive sensually by overcoming your bodily instincts that attract you to external objects via desire, and by what you seek to avoid via fear. Courage is the ability to pursue one's good intention with a foundation of love, regardless of your life experience.

One's goal should be to make each component on the model ideal. Turn the ideal into an example. If the external actions of your body are fair and kind, you overcome your body's fears and desires with moderation, courage is utilized to maintain your good intention, you focus the attention and beliefs of your mind with wisdom, and set your heart's intention toward good and acquire stillness via contemplation or meditation in order to intuit the natural laws, then you are practicing the path toward becoming an ideal human being.

To have the best conscious experience involving your reasoning mind, one should pay attention to where one's attention is directed. This becomes habitual over time. Where one's attention is directed has a tremendous effect on the beliefs one retains to inform their perspective. The ideal practice to best direct the activities of the reasoning mind is wisdom.

The exercise of wisdom allows one to move beyond the perspective of the reasoning mind and move toward that of the conscience-aligned heart. Here, the mind is stilled via contemplation by philosophers, and via meditation in other wisdom traditions. At this level of perception, one intuits the natural moral law that lays the foundation of the conscious human experience. To be an ideal human being, one needs to practice the virtues in order to achieve this level of conscious experience.

As one more habitually practices the virtues and comes into alignment with the natural moral laws upon which human experience is founded, one approaches transcendence. The primary focus here would be intuiting the feeling of unconditional love and allowing this feeling to be the foundation of your actions within the world. When one embraces the transcendent perspective and approaches their conscious experience infused with a feeling of love, one's relationship to the external world changes. Here, one is grateful for the fact that they are able to have this conscious experience here and now because they perceive the beauty in the external world and seek to create beautiful things within their context.

As one engages their external world now from a transcendent perspective, the natural actions are just and fair in general, and kind when directed toward fellow human beings. The reaction from the external natural system one finds themselves in will result in a better, more enjoyable life experience.

The pursuit of wisdom entails both making one's internal perspective greater as well as one's external context. The two main tools for doing so are one's attention and intention. As one directs their attention toward beneficial things, one retains knowledge that proves useful in the educational process by becoming aware of the relationships between concepts. By directing one's intention toward the appropriate goal, one is able to perceive the creative natural living system of which they are a part.

CHAPTER 6

Virtual Reality Ethics

Meaning

Remember that thou art an actor in a play of such a kind as the teacher (author) may choose; if short, of a short one; if long, of a long one: if he wishes you to act the part of a poor man, see that you act the part naturally; if the part of a lame man, of a magistrate, of a private person, (do the same). For this is your duty, to act well the part that is given to you; but to select the part, belongs to another.

—Epictetus

This section is an attempt to modernize Plato's cave allegory. To bring this powerful thought experiment into the information age, it would be useful to make it comprehensible to present-day human beings. Just as the cave would be a comprehensible experience for ancient Greeks to ponder and relate to, those in modern times can relate to the technology of virtual reality (VR).

VR systems allow you to put on a headset and other gear that alters your perception of reality so that you are viewing a digital world that appear real, and it both affects and is affected by your actions in the game. The updated allegory of the cave is as follows: imagine that you have put on a VR headset and supporting gear and that you are wearing those devices right now as you engage in your normal everyday life. Now, the purpose of the VR game in which you are engaged is to take the CBE model and use its relational systemic design to utilize the components displayed in the model in your real life in order to "Be Good Now."

The best analogy for the proper way to conduct one's self in life is take the perspective of your life being a video game in which you control yourself as the main character. Obtaining this objective view is critical to truly understand CBE and why it makes sense to practice. This allows for a reflective experience, so that one is able to self-reflect and think through how one chooses to proceed, and see oneself within the proper, infinite context. Such self-reflection, especially repeated regularly over a period of time, is essential for the cultivation of wisdom. As you navigate through life's challenges, the proper question to ask is: "How do I gain wisdom from this experience?" Your perceived context, received via data, is the computer environment within which you interact and create experiences. Control is what you are able to exert over data in your quest to transform data into more valuable forms.

The concept of "Role" is an important one here. Assigned roles can be used beneficially as well as detrimentally depending on how they are utilized. In a business context, one can use the assigned role of "manager" to model ethical behavior and promote unity among those employees that work for them. Altneratively, one could use the managerial role to model unethical behavior and generate dissent within their organization. For the instant thought experiment, one could envision themselves in the role of a video game character and play the game of life in such a way so as to develop as much wisdom as possible.

Imagining that one inhabits a VR game can be utilized as a modern practical approach about how to live a good life. Technology provides connection with others beyond one's more provincial perspective. Additionally, VR allows one to experience care for others via experience of their perspective. Thus, imagine life as a game you are playing in which the goal is to acquire more wisdom. This logically created role will effectuate the emotional love that philosophers had toward wisdom. Furthermore, it will provide insights into the conscious center point of self from which emotions and thoughts can be observed. This can be considered a modern version of Plato's cave. This is the thought experiment that brings to bear the full force of a three-dimensional triangle, and the final paradigm shift. After comprehending the model and its component parts, one then accepts their experience. This can be achieved by developing the three aforementioned CBE practices: nonjudgment, nonattachment, and nonresistance. And the key to these three laws are the six virtues.

The key practice encouraged by the modern allegory is to take one's identity away from their thoughts or feelings or sensations or beliefs and instead place it in a location squarely behind and greater than those component parts that are utilized to successfully play the game of life. The best approach to take in order to win the game is to treat every experience as a learning opportunity to broaden your perspective on the path to experiencing wisdom. Now, let's turn to a modern representation of Plato's cave, using CBE and VR to put it into practice.

Winning the Game of Life

Zeno was the first (in his treatise on the Nature of Man) to designate the end "life in agreement with nature" … which is the same as a virtuous life, virtue being the goal toward which nature guides us.

—Diogenes Laertius

You are the center of your conscious experience here and now in space and time. You always have been the center of your conscious experience. This is the only constant in your entire experience of life. Your thoughts, feelings, and sensations have all changed innumerable times within that same time frame. Philosophers sought to determine what was constant in the experience of life. They reasoned that this must be the foundational aspect of reality, both internally, within themselves, and externally, in the world they inhabited.

Plato determined that ideal ideas were the eternal, timeless, unchanging entities external to us, and that our soul, the aforementioned center of your conscious experience, was the timeless, unchanging entity within ourselves. He reasoned that one should educate themselves on how to connect with the ideal idea of what it means to be a human being. Connecting our eternal soul to eternal ideal ideas was the purpose of philosophy, "the love of wisdom." Love was the emotional feeling that motivated one to focus their mind toward the intention of experiencing these ideal ideas via intuition, the most ideal of which was The Good.

What one learned via the nature of their education on how to be an ideal human being was that practicing the virtues was the most efficient way to progress toward that intention. The philosophers initially posited only four cardinal (cardinal because all other ideal human practices hinge on these) virtues: wisdom, courage, moderation, and justice. Modern science in the form of psychology adds two more virtues: humanity and transcendence. The habitual practice of these virtues allows one to overcome aspects of the body with the reasoning mind and then go beyond to the emotional heart.

Three concepts can be utilized to illustrate the relationships that exists in our conscious experience: perceiver, perception, and perceived. The perceiver can best be understood as one's perspective, their point of view, or how they understand their conscious experience. This is the reference point from which one engages their external world. Perception is the film of conscious awareness that separates the internal you from the external world. It is sensual in nature from the body's perspective, conceptual in nature from the mind's point of view, and moral in nature from the heart's perspective. Context is the creative natural system of life within which we find ourselves, though we often reduce our context to a much smaller scale.

In order to control and focus the mind toward the intention of perceiving the good, the externally focused attention of the mind has to be redirected via wisdom, the desires of the body have to be moderated and one's good intention courageously maintained. Having done so, one's actions will be just (fair and balanced) in general and one will treat their fellow human beings with kindness. As one habituates these actions, their conscious experience of the world changes and they perceive their context as a living natural creative system.

You are always the exact center of your conscious experience in the here and now of space and time. You inhabit a body that perceives the world you inhabit via the senses, and your body is instinctually drawn toward things you desire and away from things you fear. In your external context, you take actions and perceive reactions at different points in space and time. Your mind allows you to think and create a perspective from which to conceptualize the world. This point-of-view is informed based on where one chooses to focus their attention and by the resulting data you choose to retain as beliefs. Your heart, which is the source of your emotional feelings, allows you to perceive the world via intuition dependent on what you have focused your intention.

As one gains control of their mind and its generative processes (attention and retention), one is able to move beyond the mind to the emotional basis of the heart. This is where one realizes they have the power to emotionally set their intention toward ideals and eventually the ideal idea: the good. One intuitively receives these ideas without the obstructive qualities brought to bear by the mind and body. The path to wisdom is progressed by learning from each conscious experience how to become more of an ideal human being, one who is good.

The changes in one's state of consciousness are what explains the different perceptions one experiences. The conscious experience of one operating at the instinctual level of the body is of a lower conscious level than one operating at the conceptual level of the reasoning mind, and this is a lower conscious level than the transcendent moral level of the intention and intuition found within the heart.

The CBE model is intended to illustrate a practical relationship between the most important components of your existence, so that you may focus them appropriately in order to have the conscious experience of a good life. If one's intention is to have the conscious experience of being an ideal, good human being, then one is capable of progressing through the various delineated phases in order to do so. One must realize that their conscious experience is equally dependent on the components found within themselves as it is to the externally listed components. In fact, one's external context mirrors one's internal perspective.

CHAPTER 7

Conclusion

Both thought and feeling are determinants of conduct, and the same conduct may be determined either by feeling or by thought. When we survey the whole field of religion, we find a great variety in the thoughts that have prevailed there; but the feelings on the one hand and the conduct on the other are almost always the same, for Stoic, Christian, and Buddhist saints are practically indistinguishable in their lives.

—William James

When contemplating the infinite external context within which one finds themselves, I would posit that the initial feeling induced is one of awe. How awesome is it that we are creatures endowed with reason and are able to choose how to behave in the infinite context within which we find ourselves? From this initial feeling of deep-seated awe, one then has a choice as to how to engage in the life they have been given. One can either choose to feel fear in response to the vast, frightening universe in which we find ourselves; or, one can choose to feel unconditional love in response to the gift of life they have received from the infinite universe and choose to proceed with that emotion as fundamental. Either of these initial choices result in the intention upon which you operate in the world. Obviously, it is of critical import which of these two directions you choose to guide you as you navigate your way through life.

The foundational principle upon which all wisdom is based is wholeness, unity, that all is one. This is true from the perspective of philosophy, systems, and psychology. One should ponder the implications of this for all aspects of life. Take business ethics: if this principle is true (and there are numerous wisdom traditions from all across the Earth that claim it is), then does it not make sense to transform the field of business ethics into as broad and interdisciplinary area of study as is feasible?

Think about this situation in reverse order. If the eternal infinite truth is "all is one," the six principles (or ones similar to them) that emanate from that ground are by necessity: wisdom, courage, moderation, justice, humanity, and transcendence. Putting these principles into practice allows you to flow with the patterns you perceive and realize the connection between your beliefs and your experience. What you believe you perceive. This allows you to choose the type of experience you wish to have (an enjoyable one) via the practice of the six virtues.

From my estimation, business ethics is one of the most vital area of education to ensure our future well-being. The general intent of wisdom is selfless integration with the whole rather than selfish fragmentation of individual data points. As one develops, the focus of attention turns inward and one's intention changes accordingly to a more selfless perspective from which one generally operates. From this intuitive perspective, one observes flow, roles, and conscience to understand how one should behave.

Each of us is capable of achieving much more than we give ourselves permission. By exercising the power of choice, we are able to interact with this infinite universe in an infinite number of ways. As we begin to choose to interact with our context in better ways, via the virtues, our experience of life becomes more enjoyable. The key is to harness our vision that presently gazes out on objects in our environment that command our attention. Once we take control our attention, our most valuable asset, we can direct it inward and note the relationship between our internal attributes and our external context. Then, we can direct our attention further, to the transcendent realm of ideas. Here, by use of moral imagination, we are able to creatively bring these principles forth into the physical world via creativity. By doing so, one's power of vision transforms the individual into a visionary, one who is able to lead others beyond the culturally hardened norms. It is this visionary individual who has the character, insight, and intention to lead the practice of business into better operations that contribute not only to the good of one's self but also to the good that is common to all.

Final Thought

A human being is part of the whole, called by us "universe," a part limited in time and space. He experiences himself, his thoughts and feelings, as something separated from the rest, a kind of optical delusion of his consciousness. This delusion is a kind of prison for us, restricting us to our personal desires and to affection for a few persons close to us. Our task must be to free ourselves from our prison by widening our circle of compassion to embrace all humanity and the whole of nature in its beauty.

—Albert Einstein

In response to Emerson's insightful quotes that began this text and Einstein's quote that ends it, I would note the following. Time is priceless. You and I are fortunate beyond our wildest conceptions to be alive and sharing these ideas at this point in space and time. Realize this. Go create a good future, one that involves the use of business as a system of good, a force in alignment with the laws of nature.

References

Ackoff, R.L. 1989. "From Data to Wisdom." *The Journal of Applied Systems Analysis* 16, pp. 3–9.

Ackoff, R.L. 1999. *Ackoff's Best: His Classic Writings on Management*. New York, NY: John Wiley & Sons, Inc.

Ackoff, R.L. 1999. *Re-Creating The Corporation: A Design of Organizations for the 21st Century*. New York, NY: Oxford University Press.

Ackoff, R.L., J. Magidson, and H. Addison. 2006. *Idealized Design: Creating an Organizations' Future*. Upper Saddle River, NJ: Prentice Hall.

Bachmann, C., A. Habisch, and C. Dierksmeier. 2018. *Journal of Business Ethics* 153, pp. 147–165.

Chavalit, F.T., and C. Laszlo. 2019. *Quantum Leadership: New Consciousness in Business*. Stanford, CA: Stanford University Press.

Collins, D. 2019. *Ethics Training: Developing a High Integrity Workplace culture*. Thousand Oaks, CA. Sage Publishing.

Covey, S. 1990. *Principle-Centered Leadership*. New York, NY: Simon & Schuster, Inc.

Covey, S. 2004. *The Seven Habits of Highly Effective People: Powerful Lessons in Personal Change*. New York, NY: Simon & Schuster, Inc.

Covey, S. 2005. *The Eighth Habit: From Effectiveness to Greatness*. New York, NY: Simon & Schuster, Inc.

Crain, W.C. 1985. *Kohlberg's Stages of Moral Development*. Englewood Cliffs, NJ: Prentice Hall: 118–136.

Csikszentmihalyi, M. 2008. *Flow: The Psychology of Optimal Experience*. New York, NY: Harper Perennial Modern Classics.

Csikszentmihalyi, M. 2013. *Creativity: Flow and the Psychology of Discovery and Invention*. New York, NY: Harper Perennial Modern Classics.

Curnow, T. 1999. *Wisdom, Intuition and Ethics*. Aldershot, England: Ashgate Publishing Ltd.

Einstein, A. 1954. *Ideas and Opinions*. New York, NY: Crown Publishers.

Floridi, L. 2006. "Information Ethics, Its Nature and Scope." *SIGCAS Computers and Society* 36, p. 3.

Gaiser, K. 1980. "Plato's Enigmatic Lecture 'On the Good'." *Phronesis* 25, pp. 5–37.

Gallon, L. 2021. "Systemic Thinking." *Sustainable Education*, pp. 830–840.

Garvey, A. n.d. *Some Thoughts on Kohlberg's 'Stage 7'*. http://glasnost.itcarlow.ie/~garveya/Stage_7.pdf (accessed January 15, 2022).

Gibbs, J.C. 2013. *Moral Development and Reality: Beyond the Theories of Kohlberg, Hoffman, and Haidt.* Oxford, UK: Oxford University Press.

Grube, G.M.A. 1980. *Plato's Thought.* Indianapolis, IN: Hackett Publishing Co., Inc.

Hampden-Turner, C. 1982. *Maps of the Mind: Charts and Concepts of the Mind and Its Labryinths.* New York, NY: Macmillan Publishing Company.

Heidegger, M. 1998. *Plato's Doctrine of Truth*, eds. M. Heidegger, Pathmarks, and W. McNeill, pp. 155–182. Cambridge, UK and New York, NY: Cambridge University Press.

Hicks, D., and S. Waddock. 2015. "Dignity, Wisdom, and Tomorrow's Ethical Business Leaders." Bentley University Center for Business Ethics, found at http:// d2f5upgbvkx8pz.cloudfront.net/sites/default/files/inline-files/Hicks%20 %26%20Waddock%2C%2021015-11%20Verizon%20Monograph%20 Final.pdf

Klein, J. 2014. "Of Archery and Virtue: Ancient and Modern Conceptions of Value." *Philosophers' Imprint* 14, pp. 1–16.

Kohlberg, L., and C. Power. 1981. "Moral Development, Religious Thinking, and the Questions of a Seventh Stage." *Zygon* 16, pp. 203–259.

Kohlberg, L., and R.A. Ryncarz. 1990. "Beyond Justice Reasoning: Moral Development and Consideration of a Seventh Stage." *Theories of Advanced Moral Development*, pp. 191–207.

McGhee, P., and P. Grant. 2016. "Teaching the Virtues of Sustainability as Flourishing to Undergraduate Business Students." *Global Virtue Ethics Review* 7, no. 2, pp. 73–117.

McKenna, B., and R. Biloslavo. n.d. "Human Flourishing as a Foundation for a New Sustainability Oriented Business School Curriculum: Open Questions About Possible Answers." *Journal of Management & Organization* 17, pp. 691–710.

Meadows, D.H. 1999. "Leverage Points: Places to Intervene in a System." *The Sustainability Institute*, pp. 1–19.

Niemiec, R.M. 2014. *Mindfulness & Character Strengths: A Practical Guide to Flourishing.* Boston, MA: Hogrefe Publishing.

Plato. 1888. *The Republic.* Translated by B. Jowett and H. Frowde. Oxford University Press.

Rowley, J. 2007. "The Wisdom Hierarchy: Representations of the DIKW Hierarchy." *Journal of Information Science* 33, pp. 163–180.

Rozuel, C. 2011. "Transcending Business Ethics: Insights From Jung and Maslow." *Electronic Journal of Business Ethics and Organization Studies* 16, pp. 41–47.

Senge, P. 2006. The Fifth Discipline: The Art and Practice of the Learning Organization, revised edition, pp. 6–7. New York, NY: Currency Doubleday.

Senge, P.M., C.O. Scharmer, J. Jaworski, and B.S. Flowers. 2008. *Presence: Human Purpose and the Field of the Future*. New York, NY: Doubleday.

Tarnas, R. 1993. *The Passion of the Western Mind*. New York, NY: Ballantine Books.

Tolle, E. 2005. *A New Earth: Awakening to Your Life's Purpose*. New York, NY: Penguin Group.

Tsar, F.C., and C. Laszlo. 2019. *Quantum Leadership: New Consciousness in Business*. Stanford California: Stanford University Press.

Waddock, S. 2007. "Leadership in a Fractured Knowledge World." *Academy of Management Learning & Education* 6, pp. 543–557.

Waddock, S. 2010. "Finding Wisdom Within-the Role of Seeing and Reflective Practice in Development Moral Imagination, Aesthetic Sensibility, and Systems Understanding." *Journal of Business Ethics Education* 7, pp. 177–196.

Waddock, S. 2015. "Reflections: Intellectual Shamans, Sensemaking, and Memes in Large Systems Change." *Journal of Change Management* 15, pp. 259–273.

Waddock, S. 2016. "Developing Humanistic Leadership Education." *Journal of Humanistic Management* 1, pp. 57–73.

About the Author

Wade Chumney is an associate professor of Business Ethics and Law at California State University, Northridge. He joined the David Nazarian College of Business and Economics in August 2014. Prior to that he was employed at Georgia Tech as the Cecil B. Day Assistant Professor of Business Ethics and Law in the Scheller College of Business. He was previously an assistant professor at Belmont University in Nashville, Tennessee, and a visiting lecturer at the University of Applied Sciences in Wiener Neustadt, Austria. Professor Chumney also spent five years in private practice before embarking on an academic career.

The primary focus of Professor Chumney's research and teaching is the *practical application* of business ethics. His intention in teaching is to present an empirical understanding of how to apply the principles of ethics in order to benefit your own life. To this end, he has created an interdisciplinary Business Ethics Minor within the Nazarian College of Business in order to teach a pragmatic approach to business ethics to students across the entire CSUN campus. In addition to a revised business ethics course, this process led to the creation of three new courses within the Business Ethics Minor: Corporate Social Responsibility, Ethical and Legal Aspects of Managing Technology, and Personal Decision-Making for Success.

Professor Chumney has been an invited speaker at several prestigious universities, including: the University of Michigan Patent Law Colloquium, ICN Business School International Business Seminar, and the University of California, Berkeley, Boalt Hall Law School Spring Privacy Speaker Series. Additionally, he has been invited to present his research at numerous peer-reviewed conferences to discuss his areas of interest. He has also received several honors for his research. He was awarded the SEALSB Young Scholar Award of Excellence by the Southeastern Academy of Legal Studies in Business. Additionally, he was awarded the Outstanding Scholarly Activity Award by the Belmont University College of Business Administration. The same year, he received a best paper award from the United States

Association for Small Business and Entrepreneurship (USASBE). He also accepted a Distinguished Proceedings Paper Award from the Academy of Legal Studies in Business (ALSB). Additionally, he was honored with the Holmes-Cardozo Best Paper Award from ALSB, the highest honor given by the academy to a piece of legal scholarship in a given year.

A native of Charleston, South Carolina, Professor Chumney has a Juris Doctor from the University of Virginia School of Law, a Master of Science in Information Systems from Dakota State University, and a Bachelor of Arts from Davidson College.

Index

www.ingramcontent.com/pod-product-compliance
Lightning Source LLC
Chambersburg PA
CBHW061835220326

41599CB00027B/5286